PRAISE FOR A*

LAB

"A.M. Revere will inspire and motivate you to understand that a person's identity cannot be defined by one's birth date or the labels placed upon them. She helps us not to lose sight of who God has made us to be. We can be set free from the labels that hold us back and discover the unique potential and purpose that God desires for everyone. This book is a must-read!"

—DAN COLEMAN, GENERAL SECRETARY OF THE PENTECOSTAL CHURCH OF GOD, BEDFORD, TX

"A.M. Revere has written a down-to-earth book to help us break free of the labels that bind us and hold us back from the person God wants us to be. "I'm so dumb" or "I'll never be able to do that" are self-imposed labels that are just as destructive as the ones we hear from others. "Boomers don't understand technology." "Millennials are lazy and self-entitled." All these labels are addressed in Revere's book, *Abolish the Label*. She shoots straight to the heart of the issue of labels and gives a step-by-step process to overcome them."

—JANE DALY, AUTHOR OF *THE CAREGIVING SEASON: FINDING GRACE TO CARE FOR YOUR AGING PARENT*

"Abolish the Label will set you free from the weight of this world, allowing you to live out your best days. As a true example of what it means to be set apart for the Gospel, A.M. Revere shares in a

relatable way how to walk out your daily life the way God intended you to as His creation, not a label of our culture."

—**PAUL DAUGHERTY**, AUTHOR AND LEAD PASTOR OF VICTORY CHURCH, TULSA, OK

"As a first-time author, A.M. Revere brings a timely message to her generation, in particular. Helping those, who are fettered with the issue of living up to labels placed on them, and how to live free of them is God-send. Her writing style is straight from her heart, which can be experienced throughout *Abolish the Label*. She's no-nonsense in her approach, yet she does so with a loving heart. *Abolish the Label* is a wonderful read!

—**TIM MILLER**, CHRISTIAN FELLOWSHIP CHURCHES, MACKINAC COUNTY, MI

"In this thought-provoking book, A.M. Revere discloses life-changing ideas to help you live out your destiny. If you are ready to change self-limiting mindsets that have held you back, this is the book for you."

—**DR. EDWIN MIRANDA JR.**, FOUNDER, SOUNDWAVE INTERNATIONAL, INC., ADJUNCT PROFESSOR, ORAL ROBERTS UNIVERSITY

"What better way to reach the youth of our day than one of their own to speak out in this present hour with the actual knowledge and experience of dealing with the labels given to their generation? *Abolish the Label* by A.M. Revere is a great read for this generation in trying to find the liberty of thought and expression as well as the real answer as to who they really are. But it is also a great read for the older generations as they struggle to understand and embrace this generation and influence it toward a higher goal. This book presents the real challenge of this generation and sets a path before them in setting an example by having an insight into what they are faced with. She deals with this subject from the viewpoint of this generation faced with a challenge as no other has had. An excellent voice to hear for all of us. *Abolish the Label* comes from the heart of that very generation. A true thought provoker."

—**H.O. "PAT" WILSON,** OHIO DISTRICT BISHOP OF THE PENTECOSTAL CHURCH OF GOD, DEFIANCE, OH

ABOLISH

THE

LABEL

ABOLISH THE LABEL

We're more than just a name.

A.M. REVERE

Copyright © 2023 A.M. Revere

First edition, March 9, 2023

Written by A.M. Revere

Front Cover: A.M. Revere

Editor: Jaime McKinney

Also Edited by: Cristel Phelps

Foreword: Stephen Shelton

Song lyric excerpt from "Ode to Overload" by Luke Cyrus, ℗ 2019 Third Coast Records III. Reprinted by permission.

All other quotations in this book are reprinted with the permission of the authors.

Readers who see this \|/ symbol, please take a moment to pray for the Grimmie family and those affected by Breast Cancer and gun violence around the world. This was written with the permission of Bud Grimmie.

Scriptures marked AMP are taken from the AMPLIFIED BIBLE (AMP): Scriptures taken from the AMPLIFIED® BIBLE, Copyright © 1954, 1958, 1962, 1964, 1965, 1987 by the Lockman Foundation Used by permission. (www.Lockman.org)

Scriptures marked ESV are taken from THE HOLY BIBLE, ENGLISH STANDARD VERSION (ESV): Scriptures taken from THE HOLY BIBLE, ENGLISH STANDARD VERSION ® Copyright© 2001 by Crossway, a publishing ministry of Good News Publishers. Used by permission.

Scriptures marked KJV are taken from the KING JAMES VERSION (KJV): KING JAMES VERSION, public domain.

ISBN 979-8-215-45067-3 (eBook)
ISBN 979-8-218-11889-1 (TP)

Visit www.amrevere.com for more information.

DEDICATION

To my momma and daddy.

To my big sis, Shannon:

Thanks for always being there for me.

1971– 2021

♡ *I love you three with all my heart.* ♡

Contents

Foreword

If someone asked you to describe yourself in one sentence, what would you say? What are the characteristics that make you who you are? If you asked the people closest to you, would their descriptions differ from your own? Who gets to decide who you are and the words used to explain that to other people? More importantly, whose words do you choose to accept and whose should be ignored?

Whether they're warranted or not, we all go through life with labels attached to us. Some of them are basic identifiers: Male. Female. Young. Old. Son. Daughter. Sister. Brother. Others are assigned to us based on stigmas, stereotypes, misunderstandings, or just plain resistance to a different perspective. The world will do its best to put labels on you that serve their purposes. They will attempt to put you in a box based on what they've known and experienced in the past. They'll lump you into a group and say that because of your age, race, gender, or political affiliation, you'll only ever be a certain way or meet certain criteria.

Fortunately, for those who are in Christ, we are NEW creations. No label that the world's system creates can contain the Spirit of God living on the inside of believers. God has called you to be an original – ON purpose and WITH purpose! We've seen sociologists attach labels to generations for centuries. In recent years, there have been labels put on rising generations beyond just their age. It's gone from a point of recognition to a place of identity. We've been told that being a millennial means you're lazy, entitled, unmotivated, looking for a handout, and destined to never amount to anything. I'm grateful that God sees us and uses different words to describe us. Chosen. Anointed. Loved. HIS.

When I first met A.M. Revere, it was apparent that she lived her life to break molds. Her passion for bringing the truth of the love of Jesus and the transformative power of the Holy Spirit are evident in every page of this book. She has truly lived this story and seen God's power in her life take her from glory to glory and open door after door for the message He's put on the inside of her to be brought to the forefront. I believe this book will bring freedom to all who read it and offer perspective for everyone in every generation. She is articulate yet accessible and offers relevant insight from a young woman who knows who she is in Christ and desires to see her entire generation join her in that freedom.

To every person reading this, from every generation, do so with an open ear to the Holy Spirit. Take a minute, open your eyes to your imperfection and insecurity, and remember that acknowledging them is okay. Even if it seems uncomfortable, every step brings you farther from who you once were and closer to who you were meant to be. We are all works in progress! Trust God to form you and shape you to match His image through every experience, creativity, and passion in your heart, and walk it out with bold and unshakable faith! This book will help you discover your true identity that shatters every label the world's system can create.

The world around us is changing daily, and the only hope humanity has is to return to its Creator and receive its Savior. I pray that this book challenges, encourages, and changes the way that you see yourself and moves you toward living the truth of who God made you to be.

Stephen Shelton
Pastor, The Bridge Young Adults
TheBridgeDFW.com

Letter to the Reader

Dear reader,

    While writing this book, I thought about some I have read myself that do not have a place where the author gets to know the reader and opens themselves up to them before chapters begin. And honestly, I think that lack is sad. I believe readers deserve to see the author's motive before they start. So, I think it's time we end that cycle.

    So, who is A.M. Revere?

    Just a random person (imagine me shrugging while I say this).

    I grew up in the middle-class world and attended a regular public school. So, I may be a student, but I am not a scholar. I'm not a celebrity; I don't have billions of dollars, and I'm not known as much. I also don't have many followers on social media, so that takes away my—what our world calls—influencer credibility. I am just a passionate young woman who loves to write and wants to touch people with her words. That's it. And a little disclaimer (that I am hoping relaxes you a bit since some books do the opposite),

I am here to talk with you, not at you. There is a difference between the two because one implies judgment on a person, and judging you is not my point. But the other means having a conversation, an informal, raw, genuine chat – that's what I'm aiming for with you. I am here to be real with you and nothing else and not afraid to be open with you. I will admit, being so out in the open is a big risk (and a scary one), but it's worth it for you. And reader, I'm here because I care about you. Because you, reader, yes, you! You have so much potential. You are unique, you are amazing, and you are a masterpiece. And you are loved. Don't let anyone tell you otherwise.

I'll never know where, when or how you found this book. It was no coincidence. This could be your destiny. What matters is you're here, regardless of where you found me. Let me give you a heads-up, what I am about to show you, might be slightly different than what you have heard. But, if you stick with me till the end, this might be one of the most incredible experiences you have ever encountered. Now that we are acquainted let's get to it.

I think each generation of our world is fantastic. Reaching back from the roaring twenties to whenever you read this, every age –their music, fashion, performing arts, paintings, billboards, sports, cuisine– is amazing to me. Every part of it adds to the richness of culture. Each attribute works together and gives off such a bright personality and uniqueness to our world.

And the fact that we are all different makes it even more breathtaking. And we are not perfect; we have our faults. So, due to this, you will find that each era has its quirks – those of my generation were Shrek trademarked food items in nearly every grocery store, Trix yogurts in split neon colors, and Tooth Tunes toothbrushes that only played one song. And oh, my goodness, ZhuZhu Pets, which didn't work properly when you rolled them on the carpet, yet I still tried. And probably the most popular but more controversial were Tech Decks, small skateboards that nearly every boy (and some girls) had and played with in school, and then the teachers confiscated them. I remember that the teacher's drawers had several of them inside because they took them away so much. No matter which generation you are from, whether you are nine or ninety-nine (and if you are past ninety-nine, I'm just going to give you a little shoutout. You're awesome!), this book is for you.

There is something I have noticed, though. In the short time I have been on this earth, there is just this one quirk (there I go again with that word. Let's just call it a problem). It's missing, but in another way, it's not. Confused? Well, I am not saying we haven't dealt with this missing thing before (I have heard it called a je ne sais quoi). But we have not dealt with it enough. And because of that, it has slowly become one huge mess. Negativity, anger, and hatred have spread worldwide so quickly. And do we detest that reality? Oh, yeah, I am sure we do. But the fact is, we don't entirely know how we got here. All we do know, however, is we have got to get past where we are now.

We cannot keep living like this. This mess has gone too far for too long, and there must be a change. I know you're tired of it, and that's precisely why I'm here. So, we have got to know. Are the labels we have heard only as they seem, or are they something much bigger? Can one moment from history open the door to change? And I know you saw the title of this book, and you are probably wondering— what on earth does that mean to abolish the label? We will get to it, I promise. In the following chapters, we are going to find the answers to those questions in seven sections:

1. **The Problem**
2. **The Scheme** (how the problem runs wild in our lives)
3. **The Fix** (the solution to the problem)
4. **The Way** (how we carry out the solution to the problem)
5. **The Vision** (where to go from there with the knowledge we possess)
6. **The Cure** (what's needed to heal not just ourselves, but our world too)
7. **The Farewell** (when we part ways)

I get it. This is a lot to see in one sitting. But I bet this will be a ride you will never forget. And if you reach the end and feel unsatisfied, you can always stop reading and put it on a shelf. No hard feelings! :)

With you all the way,

A.M.

I

THE PROBLEM

Chapter 1

When I was in school, the two brands everybody wanted to snag were Aeropostale and American Eagle. I always saw them - flip-flops, jackets, backpacks, sweatshirts, t-shirts, and sweatpants - and nearly everybody was talking about them. Whether you were a girl or a guy, those were the focus, no matter how much money your family made. And in my school, at least, if you didn't have a piece of clothing with those two brands, you did not exist. You were seen as an outcast. <u>Do you remember this time?</u>

One girl in my class, I'll call her Theresa, was not like the other students. She had worn-out tennis shoes she wore each day. She did not have the best-looking clothes, her hair was always ratty in a braid, and she even used washable markers as nail polish because she could not afford them. The other students labeled her as poor. They told her she was worthless and picked on her. And they told her she would never be able to buy anything nice for herself. But when her grandmother bought her an Aeropostale t-shirt and sweatpants, things began to change. She was accepted, and some popular kids started to compliment her. And this lasted for almost a whole week. It was a big deal for her. But you see, it wasn't about her heart of gold or her smarts that got people's attention. It was all because she was representing *the brand.* She fit in for a little while, but the change was temporary. When another fad took place, she was thrown back into the pit of unpopularity and sat with me again at the lunch table as she used to before.

This reminds me of when we go shopping. And a lot of the time, when we walk into a store, we want to find what's trendy or on-trend. Although we find something we think we like, we will leave it and keep exploring. Because although it was nice, it wasn't, quote-unquote, the brand. And that is how the whole gambit with many of today's labels came to be. It all started with a trend. Because it was popular, we wanted to follow it and, thus, belong to it (just as in the illustration with Theresa). The big picture here is like this scenario, except it is around the labels *we* hear and wear.

Since I began writing this book, I've asked people around me what they think labels are. Are they nametags? Notecards? Are they words that describe us as employees in our destined careers? Or maybe a big chunky group of put-downs? I remembered their answers and devised a way to categorize these labels. I call this first group, *Character Labels* because they describe a person and their character, whether it's about their physical makeup, status, or personality. Some are great, and some aren't. There are many more to add to this list; these are just a few. As you read them, think about what you have been told you are out of these and where you believe you fit. You can even circle them if you'd like. Remember, it is okay to acknowledge them. There's no shame in it! For example, I highlighted those I have been called in my lifetime.

• Disabled
• Single
• Prisoner
• Cancer
• Lost
• Unloveable
• Orphan
• Employee
• Timid
• Easy
• Worthless
• Abused
• Cursed
• Bulimic
• Outsider

- Hero
- Good

- Dumb
- Hypocrite
- Bossy
- Loner
- Fear
- Mistake
- Drug-addict
- Rich
- Taken
- Whiner
- Beautiful
- Victim
- Careless
- Mentally-ill
- Overachiever
- Unloved
- Anorexic
- Bad
- Joker

• Bully
• Lover
• Weak
• Forgotten
• Goody-two-shoes
• Religious
• Poor
• Suicidal
• Depression
• Anxious
• Spoiled
• Bigot
• Lazy
• Abuser

Okay, now comes another category of labels. These are a bit different than the previous list. This second group here is known in our world as *Generational Labels*. When this book was written, one of these generations had not been born yet and was upcoming. As of recently, common ones are:

• The Silent Generation (1928 – 1945)
• Baby boomer (1946 –1964)

- GenX (1965 – 1979/80)
- GenY (known widely as the millennials, 1981 – 1996)
- GenZ (1997 – 2010)
- Generation Alpha (2010 – 2024)
- Generation Beta (2025 – 2039)

While I was researching these different eras, I found something quite odd. Did you know that one of these labels, millennial, never meant what it does today back in the 1600s? Its first definition was created back in 1664 as an adjective. It was defined as "a millennium, a period of one thousand years."[9] It wasn't until 1991 that this second meaning was put into the dictionary as a noun – the one we are referring to. So, how did baby boomer, millennial, GenX, GenY, and GenZ become what they mean today? Well, they were created merely for marketing purposes. Yep, you got that right, marketing – buying and selling, all for the gain of wealth. It sounds kind of useless, doesn't it? For example, according to Forbes, the actual millennial label was coined by Neil Howe and William Strauss in that same year, 1991. It was initially defined as a person born in the 1980s or 1990s. And guess what? That definition never really stuck.[13] It has changed many times. Today, some believe the true meaning fits into the wide age gap, spreading from the 1980s to the early 2000s.[15]

So, that would be age forty to the early teen years? What? That makes no sense either! Some think it starts in the 1990s. Some think it ends in the 2000s. So, which is it? Your guess is just as good as mine. The term baby boomer was coined back in World War II. Also, GenX was put together in the same year as millennial by Douglas Copeland in 1991. GenZ was mentioned in the early 2000s, though we don't know where it came from. And finally, Generation Alpha was coined by sociologist Mark McCrindle.

Let's combine a few from the first category of labels with the ones we just discussed. <u>Have you heard these statements before?</u>

Old-fogey:
"Oh, you baby boomers are too old. You just don't understand."
"GenXs still carry around their compact discs. Get with the program. At least use an iPod!"
Narcissistic:
"Millennials are all about me, me, and MORE me."
Tech-Addict:
"All these Glass Generation kids do is watch and make TikToks. They can spend hours on the couch scrolling without even knowing I'm sitting beside them."

Okay, okay. I will admit those were a little raw. My goal is to make these as accurate to you as possible. So, let me ask you. <u>What is the first thing that comes to your mind when you see and hear these labels, whether generational or not?</u>

I wondered, too, just as you are right now, there was a time in my life. And at that time, I wondered hard. I was first called a millennial by the same person once when I was seventeen and then again by the same person when I was eighteen. It shocked me out of my boots. Oddly enough, that person was my own pastor. All I could do was scrunch my eyebrows at him and scowl. Imagine how funny my expression looked (he laughed when he saw my face, haha). However, keep in mind I was not angry when I heard Pastor Tim call me a millennial, and I have never been mad at him because of that. I also did not have any bitterness towards him or what he said. How some of us react today is how I felt. My mind suddenly went, "Uh... what?" I was speechless. But that confusion turned into questions. Instead of drawing conclusions and getting bitter, I chose to think about it and then search it out. Why? Because back then, I didn't know what to do once I heard that label. I thought I did. But if I'm being honest with myself, I didn't. Here is why.

After picking through the crowd, listening, and making observations of those around me (whether I knew them or not), I discovered that when we hear these labels (whether positive or negative), we think either one of four things or these combined.

- **Hatred** would bitterly say, "I detest that word. All it does is bash me with negativity. Do not call me that again."

This is the area where I may want to trigger a comeback. For instance, I could have said to Pastor Tim, "Oh, yeah? Well, you're such a _____! I'll never forgive you again!" Remarks like this are not the best idea (not to mention, that's not a nice way to talk to a pastor). I will explain why in a second.

- **Acceptance** can be positive or negative. Some people think being affiliated with their label is a good thing. One positive and proud response could be as bold as, "Yeah, of course, I am! Hello?" You could even go with, "That's so nice! Thanks!" Or the negative spectrum of this for those who see labels as hindrances could be, "I know I am… I will always be that way; I can't do anything to change it."

- **Neutrality** would likely say, "That's stupid, whatever." Or my favorite… "Seriously?"

- **Defense** does not have to be done by you specifically. It could be from someone who wants to try and better the situation. An example might be, "You might think that, but you don't know them like I do. If you will just give them a chance, they might just prove you wrong."

The final one is an excellent way to respond; not going to lie.

In the scenario with my pastor, I could have defended myself with a positive attitude and told him, "No, I'm not. You know me. I live a better life than that." But let me tell you this. We might think saying our opinion is all we need to do, and then we can brush it off and keep going. It sounds easy and comfortable. But the reality is, although it is hard to take, just speaking out has done absolutely nothing. Like I have said before, our world is so beautiful. Imagine flying in a helicopter from state to state or country to country. You will see the mountains and the oceans and how they glisten in the sunlight. But if you look closer at the cities down there, you will see that what lies below isn't all that reflects its appearance. Who knew?

I have heard many times, "Sticks and stones may break my bones. But words will never hurt me." Really? Then why are thousands ending their lives each year? Why are people cutting themselves or snapping their skin with rubber bands because they feel worthless? Why do they turn to alcohol, drugs, or relationships? Why are some of us so depressed that we won't even leave our homes? Think of those you love.

Your parents.

Your daughters.

Your sons.

Your friends.

Your coworkers.

Your grandparents.

You see them put on a brave face, but you know deep down they are struggling. Now, ask yourself. If you knew the answer, what would you do to help them? I don't know about you; I would do anything to see things change.

Chapter 2

When I was a teenager, there was a paragraph people on social media would duplicate and repost. Then they sent it to their friends. It challenged the person who received the message to send it to others to see how authentic their friends really are. And if their friends cared enough and felt the same way, they would pass it forward and send it back. I have no clue who created it, but I think this is one of the best ways to start this chapter. I remember scrolling through the forum and seeing reposts of this. And it immediately got me thinking. If people knew who or what caused their loved ones to suffer, they'd do anything to avenge that person. Meaning, no matter what, they would find a way to do justice on that person's behalf and completely do away with the evil behind it. The original paragraph gets a little crazy and repetitive, so here is just part of it below. Do you remember this post?

"If you were killed, I wouldn't be at your funeral. I'd be in jail for killing the person who killed you. We are true friends. We ride together; we die together. Send this to everybody you care about, including me, if you care. See how many times you get this. I want you to know you are an amazing friend till death and forever. If I don't get this back, I understand."

You may be feeling this way right now about your loved one. But I would like for you to apply this to yourself too. What would you do if you knew what caused *you* to suffer? Well, maybe the issue is people. It seems logical. Perhaps it's her. Or him. Or them. We get so tired of hearing it all shot at us. And those words can hurt. And man, we try so hard to ignore them. Let me know if you don't ever feel this way. But sometimes it seems, no matter how hard I've worked and confident I am...

I can't shut out the noise.

No matter how good of a person I believe I am or what I say, I haven't been able to drown them out myself. And I still can't because those labels are screaming loud. So loud that my voice – who I truly am deep inside – can't be heard.

When I first wrote this book, I was on my Summer vacation. I watched the sun go down on the waves of the lake through my open window, and as I watched, I was thinking about you. I was praying for you. Before this book came to be, I would go through my day, see what was happening around me, and feel something I could not describe. It wasn't long ago that I saw it in the eyes of someone I love dearly. But, now that I am taking the time to get to know you more and ponder on the things of life (ignore how cheesy that sounds), I finally see it. I finally understand. That feeling is helplessness. Let me repeat that. That feeling is helplessness.

Yep, that is exactly how I felt – I felt helpless. And I am sure that is how you are feeling right now or have felt before. I know your pain. I get your struggle. Like my favorite teacher frequently said throughout the whole year: the struggle is real. But notice something here. I said helpless. <u>Just because you're helpless does *not* mean you have to be hopeless.</u>

Chapter 3

When I think about life, I can see it as a stage, as
Shakespeare has said. I could see it as the life of a tree, and
each season it goes through. Maybe a river, always
changing and flowing. But for some odd reason (I can't
understand), I see life as a trail, an open pathway. And for
each mood, whether it is sadness, joy, or fear, the
atmosphere of that pathway changes as I walk through it. I
never thought that helplessness could have anything to do
with these labels. That was until God showed me this
illustration. Take a walk with me, and let's see about this
trail He has to offer us.

It isn't completely dark on this trail, but tiny patches
of darkness appear as the trail grows farther and farther
away from us. Before walking through it, we decide to sit
several feet away from it to see how others respond. We
watch for a few moments as individuals approach it and
begin trekking through. We soon follow. As we start
moving, only a few inches inside, we hear sounds. You
grimace and look around you, wondering where on earth we

are. I reach my arm out and halt both our strides. When we are no longer moving, we notice something about those sounds. It isn't just background noise. Those are voices. They're whispering to us that we are not good enough, telling us who we will never be. They continue to taunt you and me as we stand there. Suddenly, we see people running towards us, grouped up like locusts, through the entrance again, never to turn back. Some people are still ahead of us, arguing, screaming, and yelling at each other, totally distracted from knowing we are even there. But as we listen to the chaos, something catches your eye. You squint and see the exit of the trail. The answer is right in front of them. It is in their grasp. Many were just about to make it but instead gave up.

Okay, back to reality.

This illustration, my friends, is what I call the **Trail of Helplessness**. I will be referring to it multiple times in this whole book, so be on the lookout for it! What this illustration has taught us is this. We want to make things better. We would do anything to make it happen. So, we try to search for the person (or people) that caused it. We can't help but believe there's no reason someone isn't to blame. Although it may be unintentional, we get into useless arguments and unnecessary fights with each other and say things we don't mean. Because of this, we get so caught up in trying to get revenge that we lose sight of what caused the problem. Therefore, we can't see past that problem and find the solution. We think:

He said that to my daughter.

She said that to my son.

They ruined me.

It's because of them that he/she is so upset.

Because of them, I am stuck in this addiction.

I am cutting myself because of what that popular girl/guy said to me years ago when I was in school.

My brother/sister would not have committed suicide if it wasn't for them.

My family is messed up because of them.

It's their fault. They will not leave me alone. Oh, but they are going to pay for it if it is the last thing I do. I refuse to let them get away with it.

But when will we learn? All of this does nothing. The people in the illustration were nearsighted and could only see what was right in front of them. They couldn't possibly notice one beacon of light or glimmer of hope because they were so distracted. Time froze. It was like a metal wall, maybe worse than that. Steel, or whichever is the most robust material on earth (that might change as time passes). But unless that wall comes down, just like them – you will never be able to get on with your life.

Chapter 4

It is such a sad reality. The worst part is that if this damaging process is done just once, it will continue like a never-ending cycle. Why? Because <u>blaming each other isn't going to get us anywhere.</u> Bad things happen. We cannot deny it. They happen to those that we believe deserve it. But they also happen to good, innocent people, and it's not fair. I have often wondered why bad things happen, and I often would play the blaming game. And all of that just led me through the Trail of Helplessness. And once again, we will find the same outcome. The problem isn't solved. The void isn't filled. And we still aren't settled within ourselves.

The dictionary definition of the word enemy is "a foe, an adversary."[8] In other words, an enemy is totally against you and what is best for your life. An enemy will put anything in your path to stop you from making it through to the end of whatever you are facing. But that so-called enemy in that list there is not a person. People can play a part, and yes, they do bad things. But they are never the primary source. Look with me at Ephesians 6:12. It says:

> For we are not fighting against flesh-and-blood enemies, but against evil rulers and authorities of the unseen world, against mighty powers in this dark world, and against evil spirits in the heavenly places. – Ephesians 6:12 NLT

That is quite an intense verse, and it kind of reminds me of a Narnia book. But it completely describes who our adversary is.

<u>Our actual enemy is the prince of darkness, satan.</u>

We may think our enemy is each other because it's a fact that no (truly) good person or thing would cause harm to you. Yes, that is true. Also, there are bad people in this world. They make bad decisions, and yes, it is their fault. But what if there was yet another angle here, something more profound than this?

I know you remember the scenario about The Trail of Helplessness. Now, think about the people and us there again. We heard voices, but that still is not what we are looking for. In the illustration, the people around us were arguing and making a commotion, and an annoying one at that. <u>However, no person argues without a cause.</u> No human on this earth does or says something for no reason. <u>There is always a motive behind everything we say, think, and do.</u> And that motive, my friends, is called sin.

Yep, that motive, the main reason why bad things happen, is because of sin. Go ahead look at what my advisor and college professor, Dr. Edwin Miranda Jr., said. Here, he lists four reasons (true statements) why bad things happen. You will see how this works with what I've been showing you.

1.   We live in a fallen, imperfect world.

2.   There is an enemy out to destroy human beings.

3.   People are flawed. They are human, and they make mistakes.

4.   The enemy spreads perversion to keep mankind from yielding to the power of God that would defeat him.[2]

We know our enemy.

That is Satan.

We know our motive.

That is sin.

So, now comes the question, what exactly is sin?

Some have said it is just when we make a mistake. You might have heard this before. But it's a bit more than that. Merriam-Webster's Dictionary says that sin has two definitions.

■   An offense against any religious or moral law.

■   A transgression against the law of God.[10]

Both definitions here are valid in this case. I could write a whole other book fully defining it, and many books have been written. But simply put, sin is this. <u>Anything said or done that goes against the Word of God.</u>

One of the best examples is in the first book of the Bible, Genesis. In this account, from Genesis 1 to 3, in the beginning, when God created the world, Adam and Eve were the first humans on earth and the first on earth to sin. In Genesis, Eve was in our place. She and Adam were told they could eat any tree in the Garden of Eden except for the Tree of the Knowledge of Good and Evil.

God said that if they ate of it, they would surely die. That is a simple thing to follow, right? However, later we find that Eve was visited by the serpent, which is Satan. Satan simply got her to question what God had told her and Adam. And then Satan twisted what God had said to get them to believe a lie. She was hooked by Satan and deceived. She ate the fruit God said not to; thus, Adam knowingly and willingly sinned and ate the fruit. And that became their fate (if you would like, for reference, read Genesis 3), thus the fate of our world. But remember what I said earlier. There is hope. I am here to show you how to get past these temptations and not fall into deception.

Let's recap what we know once again.

- We know our enemy. That's Satan.
- Arguing with each other and blaming one another is not the answer.
- Our motive as humans is sin.
- Sin is anything said or done that goes against the Word of God.
- Alright. Now let's move on.

In our main illustration, the Trail of Helplessness, I want you to catch something here. There are two types of people in this world: one, those who willingly do wrong and don't care they've done it, and two, those that don't know that what they are doing is wrong. In the illustration, the people fit into the second category. They did not know they were sinning. They were hurt, angry, upset, and doing everything to avenge themselves and their loved ones. They hated what was being said to them. They were fed up with hearing those labels. They wanted a change, just like you and I desire now. But they were so distracted and blinded by sin that they could not find the real solution. Some people do things knowing they sin, and some don't realize they sinned at all. They tire themselves out arguing and blaming each other to the point that they give up. Their problem is this. They were not dealing with the sin in their lives. Thus, it was blinding them from the true answer. And if they took the time to deal with that sin and look just a bit further ahead, they would see (just like you and I did) that the way out was right in front of them.

So, where did we go wrong? And how can we prevent ourselves and our loved ones from falling into this trap? Let's see Satan's plan for all of us comes in. Then we will have the chance to expose his plan once and for all. It is time to uncover the scheme.

II

THE

SCHEME

Chapter 5

When I was first writing this book with absolutely no clue of what to do, something so random came to my mind, math class. I wondered how something so off-topic has anything to do with these labels. But then I noticed that it somehow does fit.

We were all taught how to solve problems with mathematical formulas in school. Those formulas are simple and easy enough to memorize by repetition. I still remember the Order of Operations (PEMDAS) and how to divide fractions by multiplying the reciprocal, and it has been years since the last time I used those! So, I am calling this the **Formula of Operation.** We just learned what sin is. Now, this is how evil comes to pass in our lives. It begins like this.

First, the enemy, Satan, brings an idea (or, as Dr. Edwin says, perversion) across you. This is the first variable of the formula.

idea

Then, as this idea comes our way, it becomes a thought. And without knowing, we grab hold of it. And it becomes not just *a* thought, but it becomes *your* thought.

idea + **thought**

And then comes an impulse, an urge, anything to rid yourself of that thought.

idea + thought + **impulse**

And finally, we act on it.

idea + thought + impulse + **action** = SIN

Let me repeat that.

And finally, we *act* on it.

That, my friend, is what we are looking for. Where we act is where we went wrong. And that is how sin can happen and has happened in our world. But there is good news. This good news is also where we can prevent sin from happening in our lives. Let me read to you again that scripture in Ephesians.

For we are not fighting against flesh-and-blood enemies, but against evil rulers and authorities of the unseen world, against mighty powers in this dark world, and against evil spirits in the heavenly places. – Ephesians 6:12 NLT

Satan can throw ideas at us all he wants. And some have given in. At first, this topic of marketing, trends, and fitting in seem harmless. How can doing something new just to fit in cause so much damage? I won't go into it, but you would be surprised how many ways—ever heard of the one about jumping off a cliff because someone else had done it? Following this world's trends, culture, and customs can be tempting. Satan cannot see our future, only our past. But he can hear what we say and watch our actions. And because of this tiny bit he can see, Satan uses those words and actions to try and snare us little by little.

Whether you are in your teens, early twenties, forties, seventies, nineties, or hundreds, it is the same for all of us. Satan understands that we love being a part of something, whether it is a cause, a group, or a club. He knows that we love being entertained. And he also knows that sometimes, we will do anything to get it, whether it means spending a bunch of money or even compromising our beliefs. And I am not saying this because I haven't been there; I have. But really, what has happened in the marketing world since these definitions came to be? I will tell you. We have all been categorized and bought according to what the market says and created to match us. For instance, Kyle doesn't want his Nintendo DS his parents just bought him for his birthday anymore; he wants to have a fidget spinner like Erica. And Christina over there doesn't want her GameCube to play Mario Kart anymore. Now she wants a different console so she can play Super Smash Bros with her older brother, Marcus (\|/).

As I showed you in the Trail of Helplessness, we have let one of Satan's ideas cycle into a blinding sin that didn't have to happen in the first place. Do you want the good news? They (those ideas) do not have to affect us. As I have heard one of the main characters say in one of my favorite tv shows, they can just bounce off us like BBs on a Buick. Ping, ping, ping, ping.[6] If you have seen what television show that came from, you know. That is all I am going to say about that one. Psychology, neurology, psychiatry, and all types of science and studies have sought to find what we are uncovering right now. They have come up with conferences and meetings, intensives, day camps, medicines, yoga exercises, and even calming tracks on iTunes. But here is the thing about those. Although they can be helpful, people are never truly satisfied. That is because they found the temporary. Those methods renew you, but they can never revive you. Being renewed is nice and all. But instead, we want to be awakened from this nightmare. We want a revival—of love, freedom, and hope. And if you allow it, this revival will spread around you, and lives will be changed. It will blow your mind. That sounds great, doesn't it? But here's the trick. <u>It must first begin within you.</u>

Now, notice something with me here. I am not saying our lives will be perfect. Nor am I promising it. But I am saying there is a way out. And because there is a way out, there is hope – for you to live with joy despite what you face. That is why I have written this book for you and why Pastor Edwin gave us those four reasons. It wasn't to discourage us and leave us questioning why our world is so messed up. It is because God loves us. And now that the devil's scheme and plan are uncovered, you can show others.

So, let's recap once again before we move on.

- Blaming each other because we are helpless and hurt gets us nowhere. Our main illustration for this book, The Trail of Helplessness, shows us that.
- Our enemy is Satan.
- Our motive is sin.
- Sin is anything said or done that goes against the Word of God.
- The Formula of Operation spells out the process of sin (idea + thought + impulse + action = sin), and where we act is where we can prevent sin from entering and affecting our lives.

But what good is it to warn each other if there is no way out? When we first began, one question was whether one moment in history could open the door to change. And that, my friend, is the next section.

/// THE FIX

Chapter 6

In 2018, before I wrote this book, I had just finished scrolling a bit about different generations on the web. You know, just to get some research in before I began. I saw many statistics and important and positive things, but I also saw the negative. I saw articles upon articles (upon articles!) filled with bullet points about FOMO (the fear of missing out). I saw forms of self-harm such as cutting, pulling hair, breaking bones, and reopening wounds. I was shown the staggering numbers of suicide and drug overdoses, and even medical conditions diagnosed due to constant overloads of anxiety and fear. And get this – even setting ourselves on fire? And there is no reason for me to list those percentages. We are not here to obsess about the negative. We are here to find answers and not discourage ourselves.

After nearly drying my eyes out to the bone from the lack of blinking as I searched, I had it. And knew I had to step away from it because my patience was on the brink of exploding. I let go of my mouse, dropped my pen and notebook, and pushed my rolling chair away from the desktop. My heart broke for you. I sunk my face into the comforter of my bed. I knew something had to be done. The only one I knew that could help was God. So at that moment, I asked God to speak to me. I prayed that He would show me why not just my generation but also why those after and before me are in their condition. But I had one setback. I had no idea where to start. He had shown me already that it all surrounded the concept of labels, which we learned, in the beginning, are split into two categories, Character Labels, and Generational Labels. But I didn't know what to do from there. I wrote this down on a blank computer paper:

_____ the Label.

The first thoughts I had, were, one—we could drop the label, two—we could throw away the label. Or three— we could tear off the label. And don't get me wrong. These here are pretty good because they make sense. Because if we drop it, tear it off, or even throw it away, it must be gone, right? I soon found that is not necessarily true. Let me give you another illustration. And if you are not tired of these yet, I applaud you.

Imagine you had a piece of paper in front of you, with a bold black dot in the middle. You can even get out a piece of paper and do this if you would like (I tried it myself to make sure it made sense, haha). Let's say that you dropped the paper on the ground in front of you. Now, what happens if you decide to walk away? The black dot will catch your eye because it is so vivid. What if you threw it behind you? Now comes a trail of wind, and there it is again, right in front of your face. Okay, what if you decided to crumple it up and throw it into a trash can? It would end up somewhere else, and guess what? One of these days, someone will end up seeing it. Do you see? It is not gone. We could do everything with our hands to get rid of these labels, but we will fail trying. Because labels are everywhere and always will be. Here is what God showed me at that moment.

There is no *I* in change.

Unless the Big-I dies there will be no way to move forward.

There I was, sitting at my computer desk, fooling myself. I was frustrated and sought the right word to complete the title of this book. I waited for days. I knew it had to be taken care of, but I didn't know how except for one possibility – maybe we could kill the label. As I wrote that down as a possible title, confident that it worked, I heard this scripture echoing in my spirit.

The thief comes only to steal and kill and destroy; – John 10:10a NIV

The truth is, death is exactly what Satan wants for us, he wants all of us gone because then he knows there will be no hope and nothing will ever change. We would be right back to where we started, maybe even farther back than that. And in fact, that is what many of us that are gone today thought along the road. Many that have died without hope thought about it – by overdosing on drugs, jumping off a building and other forms of suicide. But then the Lord showed me something I never knew before. Thousands end their lives each year, no matter what the age, because they didn't have God. They could not get rid of the sin in their lives. And because of that lack, they had nowhere to turn but to hopelessness. It is all because they were enslaved to this paradox. Everyone believed in their hearts:

"The only way I will be able to thrive in peace is to die in agony. When I am dead, this'll all be over, and I will finally have peace."

Man, it gets me every time I see that. If a person doesn't know Jesus and lives with sin inside them, they will always be enslaved – whether they die or live.

And though we may never understand it, it has been proven. We can and have been blinded by labels. If we are not careful, they can escalate into sin. As we went over in our Formula of Operation, sin is formed from an idea and then transforms into action through a series of steps. So, you are probably looking at the title of this book and wondering, "Where is she going with this?" Well, this is where the answer comes in.

Chapter 7

What is the opposite of slavery? Freedom. A moment in history opened the door to change, liberating masses of people. I will try not to get too historical on you, but it was during the Civil War in the 1800s, and the country was in a huge mess. It was divided between the north and south, where the south owned slaves, and hatred spread like a virus across our nation until President Abraham Lincoln issued an executive order on September 22, 1862, known as the Emancipation Proclamation.

He declared, "All persons held as slaves within any State, or designated part of a State, the people whereof shall then be in rebellion against the United States, they shall be then, thenceforward, and forever free." The House of Representatives passed it on January 1st, 1863, but it was finally ratified on the sixth of December in 1865. It is observed today as the 13th Amendment to the U.S. Constitution.[1] The men and women's bonds were broken. And slavery was abolished. This is where we are now, several decades later, just as these people were so long ago.

We didn't know it, but we have let these labels be our master. They were positioned there when we decided to carry them on our backs, and the moment we believed we alone were in control of our lives. Like I said before, death is not God's plan for us. That scripture you just heard does not stop there. There's an ending to it. Read with me the entire verse from start to finish.

The thief comes only to steal and kill and destroy; but I have come that they might have life, and that they might have it to the full. – John 10:10 NIV

You see, Jesus did not come to destroy or kill, and He did not come to steal from us either. Instead, He came to give us life. And not just that, but life to the full. <u>Our purpose with these labels is not to die trying. Instead, it is to find life in the process.</u> Life is not living in intellectual technicality and psychological mumbo-jumbo. Instead, it is life found in the reviving life and mission of Jesus Christ. His mission is summarized in these two verses. You will notice in bold what we are discussing too.

*The Spirit of the Lord is upon me, because He hath anointed me to preach the gospel to the poor; He hath sent me to **heal the brokenhearted**, to **preach deliverance to the captives**, and recovering of sight to the blind, to **set at liberty them that are bruised**, to preach the acceptable year of the Lord.* – Luke 4:18-19 KJV (emphasis added)

The second I knew our purpose was to be freed from the label and Satan's grasp, I finally wrote down the missing piece, *abolish*. That is how the title of this book came to be. It felt like I would have to go through months without having the answer, maybe even years, and although finding a book title is not a big deal at all, I believe this goes hand in hand with facing difficult things in life. Nothing is more challenging than suffering. But what is worse is wanting a solution for your suffering and not being able to find it. And that is probably what you have wondered about at least once in your life. I bet if I sat with you, you would probably ask me that same question.

How long will it be before my life changes?

How much longer until my loved ones finally have peace? Until I finally have peace?

And then, I had one question, which is one we need to answer. How can abolition, the act of being freed, become permanent? The answer is found in that moment of history – in 1865 when the 13th amendment to the Constitution was added.

The men and women could have been told they were free. Someone could have literally walked up to them and said, "You're free. Go on, get out of here." But they would still be in chains. They could even plan to try and escape but be assured someone would come running after them to bring them back into bondage. Why?

Because being told was not enough to free them.

Being told, changing our minds, or even brushing off these labels will *never* free us. It will never allow us to move forward into who we really are, the masterpiece God created us to be. What released them will do the same for us and it is found in two simple words.

Fine print.

Because once it was a law with the President's signature, nothing could undo it. This was the same back in the Bible times. When a decree was put before the king, it was not law until the king dipped his signet ring in ink and sealed the order with his stamp. Whether it was signed by the President or sealed by the king, not one thing anybody could do or say would ever change the law. Because it is stamped in, it is sealed. It is a promise never to break. And even better, it lasts forever. It is eternal.

Heaven and earth shall pass away, but my words shall not pass away. – Matthew 24:25 KJV

And guess what? We have our fine print, never to change, and the King, our King, Jesus Christ, seals it for us. It was sealed the moment Jesus won the victory at the cross and said, "it is finished." We must take our thoughts captive and enslave those thoughts in the Name of Jesus through our fine print, the Word of God. And when a thought comes across us that does not belong, we can combat that with what Jesus says about us. Only then will we have the victory.

Casting down imaginations, and every high thing that exalteth itself against the knowledge of God, and bringing into captivity every thought to the obedience of Christ; – 2 Corinthians 3:5 KJV

The first and best decision you will make to experience victory is accepting Jesus as your Lord and Savior and asking Him to come into your heart and life. So, you too will have the seal, His Blood shed through the cross, to stamp in your name as His Child and experience the freedom only found in Him. If you have not accepted Him already, I encourage and welcome you to join me in **the Appendix: Accepting Jesus**, located in the last few pages of this book. Together, we will break down the foundations of faith, answer questions you may have, and read all about how to begin living your life for Jesus. If you feel ready to, feel free to join me there!

Wow. Look at how far you have come in this short time we have been together. By casting down imaginations as we just read in 2 Corinthians 3:5, we can hold our heads high in unshakeable confidence that Jesus is Lord over our thoughts. When a negative thought comes, through the power of Jesus' Name, you have the authority to say, "No, no, no, that thought does not line up with what Jesus says about me in His Word, so I am NOT going to entertain that thought, and I am NOT going to let that escalate in Jesus' Name." That's awesome, isn't it?

Let me ask you. What have you gotten out of this book so far? I encourage you to use the open space below or grab a notebook (maybe even the note app on your phone). Write what's on your mind.

We are so close to altogether abolishing the label. Before we continue, let's once again recap what we've learned.

- Through one moment in history, the Emancipation Proclamation, we saw that instead of throwing away, dropping, or killing, the best way to help ourselves and those around us is by abolishing the label – which is the opposite of slavery.

- We find this answer through the concept of fine print.

- Satan's purpose is to steal, kill and destroy. But Jesus came that we might have life to the full.

- Jesus' mission is to preach the gospel and deliver those that are in bondage to sin.

- The seal for our Eternal Law is through Jesus and what He has done at the cross. And the first step to experiencing this victory through Jesus is to accept Him as Lord in our lives and ask Him to come into our hearts.

- Our Eternal Law is God's Word, and it will never change or fail us. And we can cast down imaginations through the power of Jesus' Name because of what it says in 2 Corinthians 3:5.

So far, we figured out the problem, found the scheme, and just now, the fix. You're almost there now.

Get ready to break those prison chains. It's time I show you the way.

IV
THE WAY

Chapter 8

Since birth, we have been taught the difference between right and wrong. We used our brains and experiences in childhood to determine whether something was good or bad for us. Typical life lessons about this may include the hot stove, what lies in the mysterious vortex underneath the kitchen sink and not swimming as soon as you are finished eating. And one favorite of mine—do not put your hand into the jack-o'-lantern because although the light is pretty and sparks curiosity, there is a hot candle that can burn you. Of course, maybe no one told me that one because they believed I had enough common sense (I clearly didn't because I burned myself as a child, whoops). Just as we were as kids, learning the way to change our generation, which is found in maturing in your relationship with Jesus, is no different. As like I mentioned before, the first step is accepting Jesus.

There is no doubt that life is very exciting, especially today. Our minds are constantly bombarded with new technology, intriguing experiences, and enlightening new ideas. Also, we can all agree that Jesus came so we could live our lives to the fullest! However, as the days come and go, we face problems. And the fact is (not disregarding the help they can bring), what education, science, and the government say don't always give us the feedback we absolutely need. This fact makes me wonder if we have ever been in a rut, looked at what these sources had to say, and thought to ourselves, "there must be more." Here is the good news. There are solutions, and even better, you are not left halfway there wondering what to do next.

Here in this section, The Way, I will show you how to carry out the solution in your everyday life. Remember from our last reading that our Eternal Law is God's Word, the Bible. And our fine print is sealed by what Jesus has done at the cross for us. At this moment, I am reminded of my favorite book by Dr. Warren Wiersbe. In his book, *Be Skillful: Proverbs, God's Guidebook to Wise Living*, Dr. Warren gives us three steps to take before making decisions in life. Dr. Warren said to *look up*, *look within*, and *look ahead*. *Look up* means to look to God and remember His Words. *Look within* means to look within your Spirit and what you have been taught (for instance, what we learned about how Jesus' words will not pass away). And the third one, *look ahead*, means to look ahead to the outcome of the decision you want to make. See the future of what it may look like and how it will affect your life.[16]

Better than education, science, and government can ever do, the Truth found in the Word is where the solution, what I call the God-fix, for each problem is found. This section focuses on *the Way*—pure, down-to-earth, trustworthy solutions and genuine fine print. You could drop the book right now and go to a college professor or even a mental health specialist with an issue. You will sit in the comfy chair and listen to what he says. But you will leave those doors still feeling like it wasn't solved because opinion is good and all. But if there isn't something true to back it up, it is nothing but a bunch of words. Here, I am going to give you some life applications. Some you may recognize, and some may apply to you. And here, you will see the answer for each of them, found in God's Word. Here is the best part about this. With God, it doesn't have to be a paragraph, not even a sentence. One breath is all it takes. And the Bible is full of His life-giving vapor. Not only that, but it is also the ultimate answer to anything we are seeking. So, let's begin.

SMARTPHONES

Is it just me, or did our phones get bigger as technology evolved? At one time, they were small as the palm of our hands, like those tiny flip phones. Now smartphones are practically as big as our heads, and some models are too large to fit in our pockets. We see these devices almost everywhere we go. It is difficult not to glance at them when they are ringing for everyone in the room to hear, and we cannot forget the internet. It all grabs our attention and sparks our interest, sometimes too often. There is a possibility most of us have experienced the product of having no sense of our surroundings. And the following key phrase on YouTube or Vimeo: "Woman Falls into Fountain While Texting" is one we may be able to relate with. Plus, it is hilarious. Look it up if you ever get the chance.

And although they are fun and keep us occupied, smartphones can be a pain as well, literally. Shared knowledge and even our own experiences show that tech-neck, vision problems, anxiety, nausea, lack of sleep, OCD, fatigue, and other chemical imbalances are all side effects. Honestly, that is a lot of issues caused by our phones. These diagnoses prove this fact: we are slowly ruining ourselves. I get it, that is a lot to take in, but that is a total wake-up call. We are putting all our time and breath into what is lifeless and bloodless. It shows in our health and puts a block on our mental state. But above it all, God is still there. He is watching us with compassion, with no intention to look away. God is constantly trying to get our attention. Because He knows the moment we do, He can bring us such a peace, better than our touchscreens can ever do. What He wants for us is to seek Him.

But seek ye first the kingdom of God, and His righteousness; and all these things shall be added unto you. – Matthew 6:33 KJV

Not second, not third, not fourth. First. If we are going to live beautiful lives while learning to react to these labels the right way, we have to make God our first priority. I have wondered why people, especially young people, leave the church as soon as they graduate high school. But then, after looking around me in nearly every activity I participate in, it hit me. Now I see why. We have got our phones out and in front of us almost a hundred percent of the time. Many in the world that are not saved don't think they need Jesus or any religion. They don't see Him as essential for their lives because they believe they have everything they need at the touch of a button or swipe of a screen. They can contact anyone they want and search for anything they might have a question about. They don't think they need God because they already have their god: their smartphones. If they have everything they need on their phones and apps, what is the use for religion? What is the benefit of God?

A few years ago, I was sitting in church minutes before service began. And beside me, I saw three people— two young adults and one middle-aged adult—with their heads down and occupied with their phones. Instead of praying, preparing for service, or even greeting the family of God there, the three were in the same pew using their phones. I honestly wish I had a camera that day so I could add it to this page. Anyways, forgive my little rant there. No hate against anyone. I am just making a point here. What will be revolutionary for us is to push our smartphones off the pedestal and instead put our *all* into Jesus. HE is your God, not your smartphone. HE is your source. Dig deep in

His Word and spend time with Him. Put Him first, with no other thing taking His place. <u>There is no pedestal with Jesus because He never fails.</u>

You shall have no other gods before Me. – Exodus 20:3 NIV

I get it. It's hard. You want to check and see who messaged you. You want to open up your emails. You want to text your friends or watch YouTube. But I challenge you today. Ask Him your questions and contact Him. Make Jesus the first thing you think about before you unlock your phone when you wake up in the morning. Give Him the last few minutes of your day before bed. Because He gave His everything so that you could be forgiven.

Chapter 9

SOCIAL MEDIA

If there was an area in our lives that would leave us up a creek without a paddle, it is social media. We can never really stand on just one side of it. On the one hand, it's great because we can contact people we don't get to be with all the time. Also, we cannot possibly feel left out because nearly every person on earth who has access to technology can see us. But on the other, we have mixed feelings because it is usually filled with articles about accidents and killings. It's like we can't search anywhere without hearing about the latest tragedies.

   And there may be a percentage of us who feel isolated, regardless of how many are watching. One day we love it, but other times we hate it. Sometimes we are
happy with it and can scroll through it for hours. But other times, we don't want to look at it for another second. We would rather close all our accounts down and throw our phones down the septic tank. Or if you're not that intense, maybe you will want to throw it at the wall. Has anyone been there before? Either way, it can annoy us. If I could describe social media in one way, I look at these lyrics to

"Ode to Overload," a profound and catchy song by indie artist Luke Cyrus.

> "I've got a lion, I've got a lion by the tail,
> I've got a weapon that could turn on me instantly.
> A dragon, a fire-breather on my six,
> Waiting for a chance to burn ...if I give it to it."[3]

Man. Look at that last line again.

<u>If I give it to it.</u>

Ponder on that. It is a question, but it is also a challenge. So, what went wrong? Well, it could be the people that post them. It could be us. Well, yes and no. In The Trail of Helplessness, we discovered that although there are bad people on this planet, blaming them and angrily typing our feelings in all caps is not the answer. And there is no way on this earth that bitterness is going to help us, it is not going to make us feel any better. So, regardless of the craziness that social media can bring to our touch screens and our lives, how can we have peace with it? You will find the answer in The Formula of Operation. Where we can stop the growth of sin in our lives falls in with this same topic of social media. It is all found in our response. How do we react the second something is put up there? The key is what we say on that touchpad before pressing the send button.

Let your conversation be always full of grace, seasoned with salt, so that you may know how to answer everyone. – Colossians 4:6 NIV

Now I get it. People say things on their social, making us want to pull out our hair. It makes us think, "Dude. Are you *kidding* me right now?" It reminds me of the one character, Bomb, from *the Angry Birds Movie*. If he gets upset or scared, he literally blows up. And what follows is anything and everything close to him. So clearly, we can't stop people from posting whatever they want. They have their own free will, and so do we.

I love how Luke Cyrus used the symbol of a fire-breathing dragon because the media can scorch people so fast that they don't see it coming, faster than a blink of an eye. But even better, I love how Luke used the image of a weapon that could turn on him. Because that's precisely what it is. If used the wrong way, social media can be a tool of destruction, from the closest friends to the best connections of relatives. I have seen that with my own eyes. Though we may try, we can't stop bad things from happening on our own. And we cannot prevent people from posting on social media. But we can choose whether they will change us. And defuse the bomb before it explodes.

Chapter 10

THE VALUE OF UNITY

I'm here for you.

If there is any phrase on earth that is often taken for granted, it's that one. I also believe it is taken too lightly and sometimes pushed aside. Think about this. Have you ever heard someone say they are always there for you but don't keep up the act? And you just want to tell them, 'Seriously, you promised you would, but I'm not seeing it,'? That can hurt. We have so many things occupying our brains today, places to go, and people to see. Of course, we are busy with life. And when we love and care about someone, our hearts are in the right place, but sometimes our actions aren't. Let me explain this. Our hearts care, but sometimes our actions don't show it. For example, let's say you saw someone you love grieving across the room. You care, of course; you have sympathy for them. But just feeling that way will not help the person unless you step out and do something about it. It could be as simple as saying to them, "Hey, I love you, and you will get through this. You're strong."

And don't think I haven't been there. I cannot count how many times I've gotten an email, text message, or talked with someone who needed me to be there for them. And my goodness, of course, we are busy with life. Honestly, who isn't? This is an issue nearly every person in our country deals with, not to mention our world. And if proof is needed, man, just look around you. But as we are so busy, we have let something slip out of our fingers – we have neglected taking time for one another.

And let us not neglect our meeting together, as some people do, but encourage one another, especially now that the day of His return is drawing near. – Hebrews 10:25 NLT

Actions speak louder than words. Instead of saying how much we care, let us lift our heads, get up off our couches, and resist missing out. Not on what, but *who* matters most. Text that person and make a conversation with them. Call them. If you are busy somewhere and can't get out to meet them, buzz them through FaceTime. And if you can see them in person, please do! Sit with them, maybe do something as simple as asking them about their day. Anything to show them you care and prove to them that they are not alone. Material things are perishable, but lifelong connections last through eternity. Live to cherish those around you as if it is your last day on earth. Don't wait, don't forget, and waste it on regrets. Instead, be the generation that treasures every single moment.

Chapter 11

EXPRESSION

God created language. He granted us the ability to communicate. Who can fathom this? He spoke, and He made the entire world. In one instance in the Bible, Matthew 4, a terrible storm was raging. The waves were crashing on the shore, and clouds of thick darkness overshadowed the atmosphere. And one simple but powerful phrase, peace be still, calmed everything in sight. But did you know God has given us authority to do the same here on earth? It is true. And one of those ways is through expression—our words.

Given that Jesus is who He is, shouldn't what we say model that He dwells inside us? Now, I get it; we aren't perfect. God did not create us as 'yes Lord' robots that can't think for ourselves. And we have emotions. Boy, do we have them! Our buttons can be pushed and that triggers an effect on us. And it makes us want to retaliate. But there is a lesson found here, and that is self-control.

The temptations in your life are no different from what others experience. And God is faithful. He will not
   allow the temptation to be more than you can stand. When you are tempted, he will show you a way out so that you can endure. – 1 Corinthians 10:13 NLT

Jesus was fully God and fully man. He was mocked, beaten, laughed to scorn, betrayed, and others even denied His existence and ministry. Still, never once did anyone find Him walking about the streets of Galilee, cursing and using profanity. He did and said everything in love, no matter what He went through. That is a lesson we can all learn from. Here is what He said about it back then.

It's not what goes into your mouth that defiles you; you are defiled by the words that come out of your mouth. – Matthew 15:11 NLT

That was greater than two thousand years ago. How much more does this matter today? God created us to use our words. To represent WHO we serve, which is Jesus. Let me put it this way. What if everyone in a two-mile radius could hear everything you say each time you open your mouth? That would be nuts, right? Well, imagine if a megaphone was attached to your neck. Picture what it would be like if you had it up to your face every time you spoke. You would be watchful about what you say, huh? Would your choice of words change if you knew everyone was listening? Now, I am not saying you have to go out in the street, put on your best walking shoes and do this. Honestly, I don't recommend it. At all.

But stay with me. There is a 99.9% probability that people will not want to be around us if we walk around using cussing like sailors and spewing profanity. And they sure won't want to be around our Jesus or serve Him either. They are going to expect and long for what is different than what they have seen and heard. We will not draw them to Christ if we talk like everyone else. We are going to push them away. We have got to watch our words because someone is always listening. Not just for our sake but for theirs. Remember. God created us to be His example for the world. We are His hands and feet, and though we may not realize it, we are His voice too.

DISRESPECTING AUTHORITY

I will be honest with you all and say that this topic is a tough one to talk about. When writing this book, the first thing I thought was to target the youngest audience I could find, which would be everyone under eighteen. However, after getting feedback from a Bishop friend of mine, H.O. Pat Wilson, he advised me in a phone call that not just the younger generations need to hear this message—the elder ones need to as well. And he was right—everyone in between and at all sides. Not knowing a thing about this, I was sure that discussing disrespecting authority should be addressed only to those my age and under. But I was wrong. Bishop Wilson was so right. It is for everybody. Because here is the deal. Whether you are one, ten, or a hundred and ten, everyone has one form of authority in their lives.

A quick example is a connection between my mom and my pastor. When my pastor was a teenager, he and his family often visited what is now my home church. My mom was the youth leader and Sunday school teacher back then. Over three decades later, God called that man to be her pastor. So the tables turned a bit. As of today, he is now her authority in the church. And they are almost twenty years apart! So, this goes to show, whether it would be your pastor, your boss, your teachers, your parents especially, your aunts and uncles, or even your government leaders. They are your authority if you sit under their wing and learn from them. And your authority does not have to be someone older than you are.

That one little *"D"* word, disrespect, often boils our blood. Can you relate? I don't know about you, but it kind of makes me want to pull out my hair when I find out I am acting that way. Because no matter what our age, the moment we say the wrong thing or in the false manner, it is implied we are being disrespectful. But the truth is, though we may detest with a passion hearing it, sometimes… we are. Sometimes, yeah. We are being disrespectful even if we might not know it. In the public eye, one example begins like this. An elderly man is going into a building. And instead of opening it for him, a person lets the door close right in front of his face. And you probably have an idea of what I am referring to—chivalry. A few years ago, I remember when I was about to walk out of a building and opened the door for an elder just about to come in. And that person was shocked, telling me no one had opened the door for him in years. It angered me. But it also grieved me. It seems that as time passes, we are letting respect for our authority diminish.

Chivalry is just one example.

Still, it is not like we did not see it coming. Apostle Paul warned us of this in the Early Church and many other aspects. Here, he alerts us of what we would see in the end times that the Bible speaks of, which we're in now.

You should know this, Timothy, that in the last days there will be very difficult times. For people will love only themselves and their money. They will be boastful and proud, scoffing at God, disobedient to their parents, and ungrateful. They will consider nothing sacred. They will be unloving and unforgiving; they will slander others and have no self-control. They will be cruel and hate what is good. They will betray their friends, be reckless, be puffed up with pride, and love pleasure rather than God. – 2 Timothy 3:1-4 NLT

We can't forget one of the most ironic places for this to be a problem, the courtroom. This may not be as noticeable when we visit because of jury duty, but we can see it most when the cameras are on. We won't go into the show itself, but *Hot Bench* is one in particular. Judges really know the law and how to deal with people. They demand respect and better be treated with the right amount of it. And if not, they will let us know without any hesitation. At the beginning of each case, a bailiff says two words that place a great deal of authority and power in their hands: All rise.

Thou shalt rise up before the hoary head, and honour the face of the old man, and fear thy God: I am the Lord. – Leviticus 19:32 KJV

Now, it's evident life isn't like an actual courtroom. That first chunk before the comma is not meant to be taken literally. You don't have to get out of your seat every time your parent, teacher, or employer walks into the room. And we especially aren't to stand rigid like trees with our nerves to the roof and never take a cleansing breath. Reread this in a version that's a bit easier.

"You shall give due honor and respect to the elderly, in the fear of God. I am Jehovah. – Leviticus 19:32 TLB

Instead, we are advised to do what is said here and treat them with respect they are owed. Because taking no time to honor these elders is not just for their daughters and sons or those in their forties and fifties. No, it is also for us aged to be their grandchildren, in our teens, twenties, and early thirties. And the point here is not just due to being forgetful but also for deliberate disrespect.

Be an example, friends. Rise above disrespect and honor your authority by dropping these characteristics when describing them—old, up-there, ancient—those are beneath us. If they care enough to invest their lives in us, we at least need to show them they made the right decision to do so. And I have no doubt we will get the same respect in return if we stick with it.

Chapter 12

CAN'T TRUST PAUL

You are probably wondering, who is Paul? Let me explain that. Back in the Bible times, when Apostle Paul was alive, he mentored someone named Timothy and saw Timothy as his spiritual son. So, in the Christian world, we call someone who is being mentored, *Timothy*. And the mentor, *Paul*. So, for instance, if someone were mentoring me, they would be my Paul. And I would be their Timothy. *Your* Paul can be anyone that chooses to invest their lives into you. If they spend time and effort helping you grow and become a better person, they are your Paul. So, now we have settled that, let's get into it.

Your mentor is your vent, your outlet to catch all the dreams and secrets you tell. They also keep you on the up and up; they are your accountability partner. As we spend time with our Paul, we begin to trust them deeply. And let me tell you. It is hard to put our confidence in and pour our feelings, hopes, and dreams into them when we feel like we are being judged whenever they are giving us advice or instruction. And don't think I am saying this without experiencing it because I have. I don't know you, but maybe you had a shaky start in life or experienced abuse, and because of that, you may take their help as a put-down.

You don't mean to take it as a put-down, and you want to change. If not this, you might feel that since you have not been able to open up to anybody, you are about to burst into a vast bubble of emotions. Or you might be tired of opening up because you feel it has gotten you nowhere but a huge argument, and you have become numb to any feeling. Hey, I get it. We were not formed to bottle things in. Have you considered this? Maybe because we are too afraid to open up because we believe in our hearts, we can't. And because we think we can't, we feel an impulse to rid ourselves of that hurt.

And to rid ourselves of that hurt, we find other forms of release—self-harm, drugs, alcohol, pornography, immorality, vaping—anything to numb these feelings. And we do all of that, only to find it makes things worse. The Formula of Operation taught us that it goes from idea to a thought, impulse, to action. We have been hurt, bruised, and scarred. And what happens from there is one of two familiar choices: fight or flight. Get up, brush off, keep going, or run to a safe place where nobody can touch us. There is a culprit for this problem, called the fear of man. Which literally means you can fear an actual person. This fear is an unseen trap. Humans are very sensitive, and not knowing how to control our feelings can tighten the knot. We wear our feelings on our fingertips because we do not want to get our hearts broken, and we all want to be accepted.

And suppose you remember what we read from the very beginning. In that case, we know that it is normal and totally human to want to be accepted and loved. But if we are not careful, that is where the fear can come in. If we feel our Paul doesn't get us, we refuse to talk to them because we don't want to hear it. Everyone does it. Whether you are seventeen or seventy, we ignore their calls and texts and let that FaceTime ringer sound until it passes. And because of these circumstances, we, in turn, put them off and shut our ears. Then, as the heading above suggests, we believe we can't trust our Paul. And instead, we trust in the only one we think will not fail us—ourselves.

These two words are your hope. But. God. Have you ever been in a spot where you have wished you could talk to someone who gets you? Who understands what you are going through and knows exactly what you need? Well, guess what? He has been there—the entire time. When you have been unsure about your future and felt like the hours were wasted without one bit of expectation or change, He was by your side and always will be. No matter what.

Don't love money; be satisfied with what you have. For God has said, "I will never fail you. I will never abandon you." So we can say with confidence, "The LORD is my helper, so I will have no fear. What can mere people do to me?"– Hebrews 13:5-6 NLT

Regardless of where you may fit here, be assured of this. God reigns now and forever, and He put those people in your lives for a reason. Do not count them out. Don't quit on them because you have this hope. If there is breath in your lungs, there is a work God has for you to do.

I am convinced and confident of this very thing, that He who has begun a good work in you will [continue to] perfect and complete it until the day of Christ Jesus [the time of His return] – Philippians 1:6 AMP

And if you don't have a Paul yet, ask God, and He will bring somebody along. And better yet, while you are waiting, tell Him! He truly knows how to keep secrets. And your feelings, hopes, dreams, anything you can think of that is yours, are everything to Him. Why? Because He loves you. You are His son. You are His daughter.

If you are surrounded by that person that loves God, take that step. My friend, God put that person in your life. He chose them just for you. And because you can trust God, you can trust your Paul. Open up, even if you are scared, even if you are unsure of the outcome. Because You are not alone, you will soon find out that they have been there too. Tell that person how you feel and what you have been going through. Ask them to pray with you and be there for you. And I believe it and have total faith in this. They will.

Chapter 13

ENTITLEMENT

When I first saw this topic, I wanted to put this book down and stop writing because this is a very pressing, tough, and controversial topic out of any of the others. Entitlement means, in a nutshell, I deserve _____, and I have a right to _____. And this one, too, "You owe me." The first side of this is logical, which is those who may feel entitled at one time or another.

"I think I have been deprived of what I deserved to have."

And it makes sense. We are human. Of course, we want things; it is our nature. And the other part of it is reasonable as well. I have heard this input voiced about others.

"I think you have been given too much on a silver platter and want everything handed to you because it came so easy before."

I get that too.

We all might expect to get our way. But there is something about this we either have already learned or will learn in the future. Entitlement robs us of any peace or rest in our lives. Those who feel entitled may one day think they have everything they want. However, <u>no material thing will truly satisfy us, no matter how much we want it</u>. We will keep being entitled and get all these things, but we will never feel like we have enough. Entitlement will not just hinder our lives and our peace. But entitlement also offends others. They will see us as greedy, spoiled people they can't make happy even if they try. So, not only does entitlement offend those around us and ourselves, but that is also still not the end of the spectrum. It also offends God.

Saying we are entitled is basically getting into God's face and telling Him straight up, nose to nose, "You're not good, and You aren't enough for me." And when we do this to Him, the fact is, we are hindering ourselves, meaning we are making our lives challenging. This is hard to take, believe me, but we must know and implement this if we are going to abolish the labels in our lives. If we can't accept the fact and believe with all our hearts, He is our King, sovereign over us, and all we will ever need, we are, in a way, denouncing Him. And it heightens from here because the moment we denounce God and believe He isn't who He says He is, the door is immediately open for unrest. If we not only believe this lie but say it with our mouths, He will have no choice but to step away, and that is when we will be in major trouble. Because the worst thing we can ever do is lose dependence on God and replace it with self-reliance.

See what Apostle Paul says about this in Ephesians, chapter two.

Once you were dead because of your disobedience and your many sins. You used to live in sin, just like the rest of the world, obeying the devil—the commander of the powers in the unseen world. He is the spirit at work in the hearts of those who refuse to obey God. All of us used to live that way, following the passionate desires and inclinations of our sinful nature. By our very nature, we were subject to God's anger, just like everyone else. But God is so rich in mercy, and he loved us so much, that even though we were dead because of our sins, he gave us life when he raised Christ from the dead. (It is only by God's grace that you have been saved!) For he raised us from the dead along with Christ and seated us with Him in the heavenly realms because we are united with Christ Jesus. – Ephesians 2: 1-6 NLT

How could we forget that we one day were sinners? We deserved an eternal penalty of judgment and the scorching fire of God's wrath. We were on our knees, afraid for our lives and our eternal future, and what we were begging for was the very thing Jesus Christ died on the cross to give us so we didn't have to bite the pain. God knew where we would be and where we would end up without the horrible torture His Son, Jesus, went through. Do not ever think that Jesus does not understand your situation. Don't ever believe He doesn't know what entitlement is or what it means to want something. He was human, too, remember?

Jesus knew the *only* way out for us was a second chance. The answer to doing away with entitlement is to grab hold of the exact opposite—God's mercy for us. And it is then that we will turn away from this lie and sin we have allowed Satan to blind us with. This reality brings such gratitude to our hearts. Pastor Paul Daugherty said something on Instagram recently that grabbed me, causing me to change my mindset about entitlement; I hope it will do the same for you as well. He said, "I would rather be embarrassingly grateful than snobbishly entitled." How thankful we are for the mercy and lovingkindness of Jesus, that He met us where we were and saved us. Be bold in your thankfulness. Reach your hands to heaven, close your eyes, and give Him the praise. He is worthy of all of it! Because, praise God, and thank You, Jesus, that we did not get what we deserved.

NARCISSISM

If there is an attribute of our world that sticks out like a sore thumb, it is narcissism. Be assured that explaining what narcissism is and finding God's answer is not one we can water down.

Pride goes before destruction, and haughtiness before a fall. – Proverbs 16:18 NLT

Now, this verse is a bit in-your-face, and I apologize. But open your eyes and your heart to see this with me. This is a very concise verse, but it is so profound and so true all at the same time. When we put ourselves first, we build a very tall structure, so who's below becomes small as a speck of dust. Though we don't want to admit it, other times, it will get to the point that we will lose our care for others. We won't see them as people but instead as distractions to who really matters: me, myself, and I. We will become our number one. We will stand on top of the weakest sediment of that shaky foundation. Then, suddenly, we will step too close to the edge. We will fall, plummet into reality, and the hit towards the ground will be *very* hard.

Just when we think the apostasy and the crash were terrible enough, we will realize it will be more difficult to recover from the physical, mental, and emotional scars we will endure. It is like that one dream when you think you are falling down a bottomless pit, and then boom! You wake up totally shocked and in a cold sweat. Ever been there? Gosh, I think about how many people on this earth allow their egos to crush them. I remember the time when I thought I was so great and that all I do is because of *me* and *my* abilities. Like, are you kidding me? I became so selfish and full of myself. What I was doing was fatal for my life as a Christian and a human in general. I was prideful. We have got to be careful that self-love doesn't transform into pride.

We just read in Proverbs what happens when we get this way and let pride get the best of us. In the King James version, it says that pride goes before destruction. Destruction. If we want to live our lives to the fullest with peace, joy, and love as we have learned and ultimately reach our goal of abolishing the label, we *cannot* let narcissism get the best of us. We cannot let it swallow us whole. So, how can we rise above this? What is the antidote for this gripping, grievous poison of narcissism? The person that said this Truth is John the Baptist, the forerunner of Jesus.

He must become greater and greater, and I must become less and less. – John 3:30 NLT

The answer is for us to decrease. And thus, for God to become greater than our ego, He must increase. Once we realize God is bigger and more powerful than ourselves, it is the moment the bonds of selfishness and getting swallowed up by pride will be broken. And then, God will truly be able to step into our lives. And He will reveal Himself to us like never before.

Chapter 14

THE DANGER OF COMPARISON

When watching those around us, it is difficult not to criticize who or what is out there. Whether you are a Christian or not, young or old, this is true for all. The moment we accept Jesus, we want to be like Christ. And that is wonderful! The word Christian literally means, Christlike. We want to grow to be more and more like Him every day. However, as we grow in this walk with God, we sometimes fight a comparison mindset. Let me show you how this works. You see, when we read and study the Bible, pray, and learn how to be more like Jesus in our everyday lives, we do two things:

1. We accept.
2. We reject.

Meaning that you *accept* the things of God because you are becoming a new person, a new creature. And then you also do your best to *reject* and stop doing what you once did before you knew Jesus. Remember, we can only do this with God's help. He is the One that changes us. We cannot change ourselves. But, if you trust Him, He will help you. It is not out of reach. It is possible for you.

Therefore, if any man be in Christ, he is a new creature: old things are passed away; behold, all things are become new. – 2 Corinthians 5:17 KJV

And as we trust Jesus to shape us and help us become more like Him each day, we notice this. Though it doesn't happen overnight, we realize we are not the same person anymore. And we are not going to fit in with the crowd. If we are not careful, we can get lost in that because we can start comparing our lives to someone who doesn't know God. If you have not already, you will see someone who is not saved doing something that is not of God. You may not have experienced this before, but be assured. The opportunity for it will come.

And though it is totally human, you will one day compare yourself to them, like comparing *A* to *B*, thinking, "I would NEVER do that! Nuh-uh! They are in sin! Red flag! No way am I going to be like them!" And if you are not careful, you will see them as a distraction from your new life, an example of who not to be. And you will view that thing they are doing as another example of what not to do. This is a tough mindset to battle.

Because when we compare, we become built up in how right standing, or how righteous, with God we may think we are. Meaning we think we've got it going on. Christian and secular culture calls it *holier than thou*. And let's be honest with ourselves. Feeling superior makes us feel good. And it is okay to admit that. There is no shame in it. <u>There is never any shame in acknowledging the truth.</u> We have all been there. Thinking we are better than others makes our flesh happy (you may remember this in our section on narcissism). Because our makeup as humans is based on the carnal.

Carnality is defined in Merriam-Webster's Dictionary as "relating to or given to crude bodily pleasures and appetites."[7] Meaning, it is all based on our five senses. Popular culture and the media have tried their best to prove that it is essential to live for what gives us pleasure. In a nutshell: if it feels good, do it. If it doesn't, don't. In a commercial for a popular sitcom called *Good Trouble*, one character said, "Sometimes you have to do wrong to make things right." [11]

But you see, this is not what faith is. Faith is about so much more than this.

Believing in Jesus is not all about pleasure and doing what makes us feel good. Loving Jesus is not about building ourselves up above others. And on the contrary, it is not about thinking we are less important either. We were not adopted into His family, the family of God, to shun everyone that isn't like us. Sure, the person may be in sin. They might not know Jesus. But that does not give us an excuse to hate the person. And it does not give us an excuse to believe we are better than them because the truth is this. I'm not. You're not. None of us are.

For there is no respect of persons with God. – Romans 2:11 KJV

He has no favorites! I feel like God wants you to know this. If you grew up in a society, a school, or a home with hierarchies and favorites, maybe you always felt like you weren't good enough; I want you to know this. <u>No matter what we do, Jesus loves us all the same, every person on this earth.</u> Because we have all sinned, we have messed up and done wrong. He sees us all the same. <u>We don't have to earn our keep with God. We don't have to do anything to show Him. He already loves and accepts us and always will no matter what.</u> I know it is hard not to compare. I used to think I was better than other people. I compared a lot. Because I was different, I did everything I could to be nothing like other people. I was so stuck trying to be perfect that I stressed myself out and just became frustrated. And I saw them as examples of who not to be too. But here is the best news ever! You don't have to stay that way.

Remember what we learned earlier. Just because you are helpless does *not* mean you are hopeless. You, too, can rise above comparison. You can be better with God's help. So, how can we fight comparison? By loving others how Jesus loves us. We see each other equally. Not as examples and not as distractions and not someone to turn aside. We see each other as who we are—broken people who need Jesus to save us and put us back together. No matter your age, gender, or creed. We are all men, women, people who desperately need Jesus. Jesus came to earth to show us the way to Him. So even now, Christ is calling us to do the same.

Pay careful attention to your own work, for then you will get the satisfaction of a job well done, and you won't need to compare yourself to anyone else. For we are each responsible for our own conduct. – Galatians 6:4-5 NLT

Apostle Paul once again is advising us. But please do not take this the wrong way. God is not telling us to pick ourselves apart with a fine-toothed comb and strive to be perfectionists. We will never be perfect. That truth alone freed me! And remember, it doesn't happen overnight. Instead, we are to trust the only One who can help us, the Refiner, Jesus Christ. There He can begin, sustain, and complete a work in us because He has called us all to do something extraordinary in our lives. Before we can pursue to help others, we must first be willing to be His vessel, and from there, He will show us. He will reveal what parts of ourselves are lacking or aren't equipped with strength, aspects of our lives that need help. And He will show us how to fix them. And He will buff those areas in our lives we are doing well in, and then we can exercise them and become even stronger. But first, we must release independence and lay ourselves on the altar before Him in complete surrender. We have got to let go and let God.

Chapter 15

So, wow. That was some intense stuff. But tell me, do you feel better now? Maybe a little more confident? Now you no longer must drown in hopelessness. You can rise above! Glory to God! Who you truly are in Christ is more than you could ever imagine. Before we continue, let's recap what has happened so far. Just earlier, in the last few chapters, together:

- You and I answered this question: "Is there a way out of the hurt and unrest we can experience from being labeled?" We found out there is, and not only is the way out possible. It is also free and available.
- We broke down one moment in history, the Emancipation Proclamation, and uncovered how being genuinely free, abolishing the label, is done.
- We learned that the truth of fine print carries out abolition (the opposite of slavery), and ours is the Word of God. God's Word, our eternal law, will never change or fail.

- We discovered our fine print is sealed by what Jesus did at the cross, and it is all ours to take. If you joined me at the back of the book and accepted Jesus in the appendix, you took hold of that eternal law and promise Jesus has for you.
- We uncovered the God-fix, meaning God's answer to typical life situations. From cell phones to social media and life skills such as respect and unity, we broke each topic down and dug deep into what God says about each one.
- We found how we can rise above the negativity and unrest labels can bring. We also learned that it is not a one-time deal, we cannot promise perfection, and change does not happen immediately. We must trust God to help us. But, above all, we know the process is rewarding because we can live lives of peace, joy, and love despite what we face.

Be encouraged. You are almost there. You can throw those chains off you and run in just a moment because we are so close that they're losing their grip if you look down. They're shaking. There's one final seal to stamp, and then golly, you're free, and it's all about one of the biggest questions you've wanted to know the answer to ever since you picked up this book.

Chapter 16

WHAT SHOULD I DO WHEN I'M LABELED?

If you remember from the beginning, I showed you that not all labels are bad. Some are good and describe you and your personality and can build up your confidence. But on the other hand, some are not so good and can taunt you, crushing your self-worth. Whether positive or negative, labels are labels; let's be honest. And just like we did earlier, we can take any label that comes at us and apply the Word of God to them, which is our fine print. But it doesn't just stop there. We can do more than find scripture for each. We truly abolish the label when we believe and speak out of our mouths what God says about our situation, found in His Word.

And since we have the same spirit of faith, according to what is written, "I believed and therefore I spoke," we also believe and therefore speak, knowing that He who raised up the Lord Jesus will also raise us up with Jesus, and will present us with you. For all things are for your sakes, that grace, having spread through the many, may cause thanksgiving to abound to the glory of God. – 2 Corinthians 4:13-15 NKJV

It works like this. We believe in Jesus, and we have faith. And because of that faith in what Jesus has done at the cross for us, we believe that when we speak His Word our situation will change. <u>So, when we are labeled, the best thing we can do is find scripture based on it and speak the Word over it.</u>

Something similar happened in the Bible during the days that Jesus was on earth. Jesus was on the road when the man approached Him. This man was a Roman centurion and had a servant back home who was paralyzed and in terrible condition. This servant's mind was constantly bombarded with terror. Ever been there before? Well, in this true story, Jesus offers to go over to the centurion's home and heal his servant. That sounds like a great plan to me. If Jesus told me He would come to my home to heal my loved one, I would say yes without hesitation. I'd be like, "Yeah, sign me up!" However, this is what the centurion says to Jesus instead. I love his response. You can read more about this in Matthew 8, starting in verse five.

The centurion answered and said, Lord, I am not worthy that thou shouldest come under my roof: but speak the word only, and my servant shall be healed. – Matthew 8:8 KJV

My goodness. This man believed so strongly and had so much faith in who Jesus is and what He could do. So much that he told Jesus all He needed to do was say the servant was healed, and that would be enough!

When Jesus heard it, He marveled, and said to them that followed, Verily I say unto you, I have not found so great faith, no, not in Israel. And Jesus said unto the centurion, go thy way; and as thou hast believed, so be it done unto thee. And his servant was healed in the selfsame hour. – Matthew 8:10, 13 KJV

Notice how Jesus responded there. He told those around Him how great faith the centurion had—not faith in himself and what he could do. But instead, faith in who Jesus is and what HE can do. And because of this faith and because the centurion believed, Jesus said it would be done, and the servant was healed the moment it was said. Amen! Jesus did not have to follow the man to his home for his servant to be well. All that was spoken was a word—a Word combined with faith. And because of that faith and that simple word from Jesus, the situation changed. When I look at people hurt by these labels, I see them just as the servant was; stuck, unable to move, and deeply troubled. And I honestly see them as afraid that they will never be able to rise above it and will always be that way. You know that saying, "sticks and stones may break my bones, but words will never hurt me," we saw this earlier. But that is a complete crock. Because they do, they paralyze us and make us believe that we will never live past them.

But, my friend, you know the Truth. You have the way out. You can rise above any label that comes your way, any hurt or scars. You have the key to unlock those chains. And you have your eternal law, the fine print that seals and secures your freedom. And it is found in Jesus, what He has done for you at the cross, and in His Word.

Make that specific verse your own, and make it personal, thanking Jesus for it. You can even add your name in there if you want! So, let's take a few labels from the list we saw at the very beginning and do just that, speak the Word only, and declare it over our lives. The scriptures are in *italics*, and you will see the sample declarations I've made for you are underlined. However, you can make your own if you would like! Say it out loud. Refuse to believe the lies. Make that Word your own and make it personal. You can do this for any label you hear.

- **Weak**

He gives power to the weak and strength to the powerless. – Isaiah 40:29 NIV

I thank You, Lord, that You give me power and strength at this moment. I am strong, in Jesus' Name.

Then he said to them, "Go your way, eat the fat, drink the sweet, and send portions to those for whom nothing is prepared; for this day is holy to our Lord. Do not sorrow, for the joy of the Lord is your strength." – Nehemiah 8:10 NIV

I am not weak. The joy of the Lord is my strength.

▪ Ugly

But the Lord said to Samuel, "Do not consider his appearance or his height, for I have rejected him. The Lord does not look at the things people look at. People look at the outward appearance, but the Lord looks at the heart. – 1 Samuel 16:7 NIV

I am not ugly. God doesn't see me because of my appearance. What matters is my heart. And my heart is full of Your love, Jesus. So, because of You in me, I am handsome /beautiful.

▪ A Mistake

You watched me as I was being formed in utter seclusion, as I was woven together in the dark of the womb. You saw me before I was born. Every day of my life was recorded in Your book. Every moment was laid out before a single day had passed. – Psalm 139:15-16 NLT

I am not a mistake or an accident, and I have a purpose in You, Lord. You knew me and my whole life's plan before I was born. Because of You, Jesus, I matter, and my life is precious.

■ **Poor**

Fear the Lord, you His holy people, for those who fear Him lack nothing. – Psalm 34:9 NIV

But my God shall supply all your need according to His riches in glory by Christ Jesus. – Philippians 4:19 KJV

<u>I thank You, Lord, that I love You, and I am Your child. And I declare, I lack nothing in life. I thank You that you provide for my every need! I am not poor and I have all I need in Jesus' Name.</u>

Do you see how this works now? Like I said before, you can do this anytime. And just like the centurion, when you find the verse that speaks to your situation, read it and speak it out believing in faith, your situation will change. Your spirit will rise out of despair. <u>You can stand tall against anything that comes your way because Jesus has empowered you to stand.</u> No matter where you find yourself in life, whether now or years later, you can encourage yourself in the Lord when no one else will.

And David was greatly distressed; for the people spake of stoning him, because the soul of all the people was grieved, every man for his sons and for his daughters: **but David encouraged himself in the Lord his God.** – 1 Samuel 30:6 KJV (emphasis added)

It changes our perspective to read a verse or chapter of scripture that gives us the answer to what we are going through. This truth makes us feel better because we know God is there for us and has given us help. What a wonderful reality this is! All glory to Jesus for giving us His Word!

V
THE VISION

Chapter 17

When I first began writing this book, I was a girl with a fiery passion. I had just turned eighteen and graduated high school. I had just started bible college that Fall and I remember watching lectures and reading material that made the Word of God come alive to me. There would be times the words jumped off the page. I was bright-eyed and bushy-tailed, let me tell you. I was so excited about learning about God's Word. I had heard my professors and other students testify that what they read in the Bible gave them a vision for their future and motivated them to continue in life.

And as they continued to step out in faith and trust God, He moved in their lives and changed them for the better. And they were left in awe of the greatness of Jesus and were never the same again. What they remembered was not the promise they received or the things they gained. But instead, they remembered Jesus. He was the Name they repeated. And as I was asking God what to write in this book for you, I wanted **you** to experience that same joy and impact I had seen others speak of. As I was sitting alone, brainstorming and asking God what to do, He gave me a vision. My goodness, it was so quick, like a flash. But it was so vivid all at the same time. I knew I had to share it with you. Here is what it was:

"In one time-lapse, I saw people young and old of all creeds, wearing a nametag scribed of all labels. Each person lifted their arm, gripped the nametag tightly with their fingers, and vigorously tore it off, ripping them up into pieces. A powerful Hand then lit a match, not with sandpaper as usual, but with the actual pages of the Bible. The blazing fire that ignited the match was of the Holy Spirit. The flame made contact, and the pieces were burned and consumed into a pile of ashes, signifying a permanent end. Each person abandoned the embers and entered daylight, walking out in the complete victory of no longer being enslaved to who they once were, but instead knowing their identity, found in Jesus Christ."

Through the time we have spent together, breaking down the surface of these labels and digging deep to uncover the answers, we know we are more than what they limit us to. We have seen just a few examples of how God sees us and how to live better lives. But now we are at the point where it is difficult not to wonder what exactly God has for us, which means the vision He has for each of us as individuals. Think of a blueprint. To the highest degree, every tiny detail is laid out. It shows the artist how to construct each piece and where they must be placed in their designated spots.

This is the same for us. God has a specific, personalized vision, a plan for me and you. And if you remember from what we read in Psalm 139, He had this plan thought out before we were even born! Not one of us has the same plan either. We are all different and unique in the way God made us. Just like it did for those at my Bible college, the vision God gives every one of us motivates us to continue and press towards what lies ahead. If there were a verse in the Bible that best represented this, it would be this verse.

And the Lord answered me, and said, Write the vision, and make it plain upon tables, that he may run that readeth it. – Habakkuk 2:2 KJV

I will never forget something my professor, Roland Depew, said about this. He said,"Write your vision, make it clear, like a billboard, so you can run by it and still see it. Though it may tarry, wait to see the result. Walk by faith, and not by sight."[5]

Without our vision, we will not be able to run and tell everyone what is to come. But I have good news for you, that crazy paragraph I have given you at the top of the page is just one vision. Where God sees you personally is above and beyond that, beyond what any person on this earth could think up. Remember. God has a special calling, chosen and picked out just for you! In his powerful message, *You Were Born to Fly*, Pastor Paul Daugherty says, "You need to see God's vision for your life because He sees potential in your future!"[4]

Without our model, which is the Word of God, we won't have the strength for the best yet to come. And that is the change we have been earnestly seeking the Lord for. That is the future Jesus holds for us. We are another step closer. Try to grasp with me what is waiting for me and what is waiting for *you*. After seeing your life revive and change for the cause of Christ, where you stood in your past, will not even matter compared to the joy you will feel. It is obvious there will be opposition. However, do not listen to those voices. They will try and persuade you to turn back. If not now, it will be later. But let the Word of God speak louder. It does not matter if they say we can't do anything because we are uneducated.

It doesn't matter if they tell us we are too young or too old. They will even say we are nuts for following someone invisible to the human eye. They will do their best to deceive us with the lie that it is okay to give up. Some will even say nothing is wrong with straying and living a little if we don't get drawn in. Let me advise you from experience. Please do not listen to them. Know who you truly are. Dig deep into the Word of God. Believe in faith that you will not quit because Jesus never gave up on you, even while He was on the cross.

Chapter 18

Imagine that.

While Jesus was suffering in front of everyone on the cross, in desperate pain and agony, He never gave up on you. Even while people mocked Him. I sure could not bear it. If I were Jesus at that moment, I would be like, "Nope! I'm done; I'm leaving. See ya!" It would have been over like green on grass. Done. Kaput. Jesus had the choice. He could have come down from the cross if He wanted to. Jesus was the Son of God, after all! He could have ended it then and there. But He still didn't. Why? Because He knew His purpose there. Regardless of the mockery and excruciating pain as He hung there for hours, He knew the price He had to pay was for the greater glory of God. It was for you and me.

So, He did not give up. His reward, our reward for His sacrifice, was greater than whoever and whatever was against Him. It was greater than the adversity. And that motivated Him to continue and press on. And I know we don't mean to give up. We are human! That is our nature!

As we learned earlier, we daily fight what our flesh wants to do. Clinging to and succumbing to things of the world while trying to hold on to your faith in Jesus is called **double-mindedness**. It's living two separate lives all at once. It can seem harmless at first, but it can be so dangerous. More than you and I combined will ever be able to comprehend.

A double-minded man is unstable in all his ways. – James 1:8 KJV

Meaning that nothing a person does will be stable if he is double-minded. Everything he does will be shaky. That is a scary thing, isn't it? The concept of double-mindedness reminds me of one of the most captivating movies I have ever seen about a man named Philippe Petit, called *The Walk*. In the movie, this man prepared to walk on a tightrope between the two towers of Notre Dame Cathedral in Paris, France. As the man walked the rope in the movie, it had me on the edge of my seat because if he leaned too far to the left or the right, he would fall. And the fall would be long and terrible. It would cost him his life. Thankfully, that did not happen, and he safely walked through to the other side. But think about it. Double-mindedness is just that, instability: leaning on one side and then the other.

When a person is double-minded, they expand themselves to live two lives—a sinner and a child of God– and go back and forth, from light to dark, dark to light. If you think about it, it is not just like walking a tightrope. It is also a lot like a rubber band. As it stretches over time, it will seem like things are okay at first; maybe we can handle the stretch. Perhaps it won't hurt us. A slight bit, a little taste, and a little sin can't be bad. But without knowing what we are doing to ourselves, if we continue living double-minded, we will grow weak. After being pushed to our limit, we will lose our strength and break, just like that flexible object after being used past its ability. And what are we left with? Not just a useless piece of rubber but also a broken life.

But you, my friend, have hope. You have Jesus. So, you, too, can rise above it. If this matters any, I am doing it, too, daily. And I get it. It is not easy. And yeah, we are not promised perfect lives. It is a process we will have to continue until the day we see Jesus in Heaven. But I still choose to abolish the label every day of my life. And sometimes, I fail. And that is okay. I continue to read the Word of God. I speak it over every situation I can. And friend, I pray for you to do the same. I pray you continue. Press on, my friend, regardless of imperfection, and praise God in the process. Thank Him that He is leading you through. My friend, I want you to know. If you have gotten nothing from this whole book, please don't forget this. ***You are not alone in this journey.***

And better than any person on earth can, God, Jesus, the Holy Ghost, and an entire army of angels have your back. Don't give up. Be encouraged.

I discipline my body like an athlete, training it to do what it should. Otherwise, I fear that after preaching to others I myself might be disqualified. – 1 Corinthians 9:27 NLT

Hold onto this promise. Whether Jesus is feet away or miles ahead, the journey will always be worth it because God has better things in store. I encourage you once again to use the space below. Ask the Lord what vision He has for you. Write out your prayer to Jesus below. Or posture your heart toward Him today and ask Him!

VI

THE

CURE

Chapter 19

You have made it this far. Now nothing is holding you back. Let this absorb and wash over you. You are free. Run, and run with all your might! Take a lap around your couch or the room if you like, and start praising God for your freedom! There aren't any extra chains cutting off the circulation of your potential. You don't have any more restrictions to prevent you from seeing the way out. Together, we have used the power God has given us to expose and burn down the enemy's schemes. You also have your fine print, God's Word, which makes your freedom eternal because it is in Jesus alone. It is the key to unlocking any door keeping you from everything God has for you. Now you know what it takes to bring change in yourself. But it doesn't stop there. And as you expected from the very beginning, you can do more than just help yourself. Whether you have been reading this book in one setting or for a couple of weeks (sometimes I read books for months to grasp them fully), my prayer is that your Spiritual ears have been open. And I pray the fog of sin and shame that kept you from seeing the answer is now cleared. We are so close to the end of our journey together. And it is almost time for me to say goodbye. So, let's reflect on all we've done together and learned.

In the previous section, in the vision we saw, you will notice that the match was sparked with the pages of the Bible, and it created a Holy Ghost blaze. And this power feeds from the Word of God. I still get chills thinking about it because it is so amazing, beyond my own comprehension. In the past few chapters, we have learned that the Word of God burns down things in our life, such as narcissism, hate, and fear. We can use it to burn down any temptation to sin or deception that will come our way as we all grow and mature in Christ. But the power of the Holy Spirit, found in the Word of God, also restores. It fixes what once was broken and fills every void and empty space in your heart you once had. So, now we have the opportunity to let that Holy Ghost Fire restore and strengthen us. Not only for today but for the rest of our lives. <u>Remember, though, that this fire is not a one-time thing.</u>

We don't go to the Word of God once a week and just pray then and then boom; we are good for the week. It does not work like that. No, this has got to be a daily thing. <u>If we are going to continue to grow as children of God and increase our love for Jesus and be more like Him, we have got to keep the fire burning.</u>

Study this Book of Instruction continually. Meditate on it day and night so you will be sure to obey everything written in it. Only then will you prosper and succeed in all you do. – Joshua 1:8 NLT

Just as we constantly need heat to keep us from freezing to death, we need to feed ourselves with the power of the Holy Spirit, the Word of God, to sustain us in the journey ahead. We need Him to keep us going and motivated to live life. Without Him and His Word, we will be right back where we started, hopeless and down. Don't let yourself lose that love, joy, and hope in Christ. Keep that Fire burning! Reflect on each of the scriptures we went over since the beginning of this book (in order from the old to new testaments), and skim through them again and again, as many times as you want to read the scriptures we covered. And when you do, feed on these words and let them travel deep inside you. If you would like, so you don't lose sight of them when you read the Bible, find each of these verses in your own Bible and highlight them with your favorite color highlighter. That's what I love to do when I see one that blesses me. And it sticks out among the other verses on the page, so I can find it and reread it.

Each verse we read and covered in this book is a good chunk of the Bible to get us started. And sure, we may think we only have a small piece left to look at. But there is good news. No, scratch that. There is fantastic news. The Fire is always burning. You can use many other scriptures in the Bible; these are just a few. This small amount you have been given, plus a thousand times that will never satisfy you. You will always be hungry for more because we can never have enough scripture. You will find that is true as you read the Bible for yourself.

Chapter 20

Every attribute of your Christian walk—reading and studying the Word, attending church, prayer, and building a relationship with God—works together to be your Spiritual lungs. These are what keep your born-again Spirit alive and your faith thriving. Just like in real life, no matter if we try an oxygen tank or CPR, no person on this earth can make us breathe. We must choose to inhale oxygen, expand, and contract our organs. If we don't work to remain consistent and in tune with the word of God, our faith will diminish, and we will start to spiritually suffocate ourselves. That is *only* if we do not supply ourselves with this life-giving Word, the Bible. It will take time to build our desire to read God's Word every day, especially when we would rather do what our flesh wants.

Sometimes, instead of reading the Bible in my morning devotions when I wake up, I have wanted to unlock my smart device and look at my emails. Still, I shouldn't because God is my priority, and it is my honor to put Him first, which means thanking Him for the day and reading my morning devotions. Because here is the deal, something you will learn as the days go on. Our flesh is stubborn and can be a pain, hypothetically and literally. But there is good news! As we keep feeding ourselves in the Word, and once we realize it is our life supply, it will become what we will long for more than anything. We will not only want to renew our minds with the washing of the Word, as it says in scripture, but we will begin to crave being with God. We will want to hear it everywhere and become passionate about its effect on us.

For the world to follow the Light of Christ in us, we need to carry it around. And not a little sparkler. We are talking about a brilliant torch that others will have no other reason but to follow. And the way for us to do that is in the very lives we live. Your generation, mine, and those around you are all infected with a pandemic that is quickly spreading. But guess what? We have the cure. And His Name is Jesus Christ.

VII
THE
FAREWELL

Chapter 21

Congratulations. We are at the final chapter, and it is time for us to part ways. Since I began writing this book, my earnest prayer is that the pages before have inspired you. One of this book's most significant purposes is to introduce you to a higher calling towards something greater–Jesus Christ. I hope and pray that has been successfully done for you.

Brethren, I do not count myself to have apprehended; but one thing I do, forgetting those things which are behind and reaching forward to those things which are ahead, I press toward the goal for the prize of the upward call of God in Christ Jesus. – Philippians 3: 13-14 NKJV

Remember that these changes we are making in our lives are a challenging feat. But as we walk in this new freedom of knowing our identity, sons and daughters of the King, people will see a difference in us. And change does not have to stop with you. You can do more than just help yourself. Because until others become saved themselves and accept Jesus (which is found in the appendix if you have not yet), they will never know what exactly is inside us. But here is the cool thing about it. It will not matter to them if they don't know yet. They'll just want whatever you have got. And that, my friend, is your chance.

This new skin, this Christlike, divine purpose, is now a whole new complete vision of the entire world, every face we see as we walk this earth to fulfill the mission God has given each of us. Now that we have been transformed and renewed, we will begin seeing the world just as God did before we called on Him. We won't see others as where they stand and the mess they are in. But instead, we will see them as the man or woman of triumph they could be if they just call on Jesus. You will look back years from now to the life you once had and the person you have become: the brave, Bible-believing, spirit-fire, blazing warrior of God you were created to be. That transformation will become your testimony, the very thing you will use as you tell others about *their* identity. Because, deep inside, we all know. That is not who we are. <u>We're more than just a name</u>.

We walk the streets, where crowds lift up their cause each day, burning national flags, boycotting landmarks, and believing good is the new bad (as you may have heard in the media lately). If we do not take a stand for what is right, it will come to the point that they will slap tape on our lips, shut us up and push us to sit in a corner. You and I, were not meant to stay there and watch our friends, family, and loved ones fall into an incoming pit of destruction when they least expect it. We were created to warn them of danger and stick a red flag in their path that can save their lives. And that is why I wrote this book. What you have just read was not about a life-changing phenomenon that only takes effect if a set of steps is followed. That is ridiculous. Instead, this book was merely a call—a call to action. You have seen the difference with me and how to act upon it. <u>Now, continue in that faith. Don't ever stop.</u>

I want you once more to think of that dark, eerie trail we saw much earlier, the Trail of Helplessness. And now, I want you to look at it with your new filter of vision you have uncovered through Jesus. My young adult pastor and foreword writer, Stephen Shelton, calls it the filter of faith. In his sermon, *The Filter of Promise*, he said, "What is fact in front of you is NOT as true as the promises of God. You have got to see God's promises through the Filter of faith."[14] So true. Man, that is so good. Sift every area of your life with that filter of faith. Choose to see everything around you with joy, selfless love, and positivity. See it as Jesus sees you! What culture says about you, your health, or whatever you are facing does not even compare to what God says in His Word. His truth speaks louder than what the world says because His Word is your eternal fine print, never to change and never to fail. Now it is YOUR turn. Walk down that trail of the unknown with the knowledge you now possess. It doesn't look so scary now, does it? I once heard a quote that has challenged me and inspired me. It asked, "What would I do if I wasn't afraid?"[12] However, you know how to combat fear. You know what you know now. You have faith, you have hope, and you are loved. You know what is possible. So, let me switch that question up a bit.

You're not afraid, so tell me. What are you going to do?

Join me. Take that step. Visualize your city, state, and even country, transform. Arise. This is your day to stop letting demeaning stereotypes define you and those around you. What do you have to lose? Fight for your future. It does not matter what others may say. You have Jesus. So, you have what it takes. Now is your triumphant hour. Together, let's abolish the label.

Hey, friend! Thank you so much for reading *Abolish the Label*!

For more, visit www.amrevere.com/.

You are known, you are not forgotten, and you are LOVED by your Creator!

Appendix: Accepting Jesus

Hi again, or if it is for the first time, welcome. I'm A.M.; it's nice to meet you! You know, it makes me wonder how you got here. Possibly you were once saved before and realized you hadn't re-dedicated yourself. Maybe you are already right with God, and a voice—His voice —moved you to give yourself a clean slate before continuing. Or perhaps you read the entire book to see where it would end before you decided to turn here. Well, whatever method it took for you to make your way since this book was first written, I have been praying you would end up here somehow. And if you don't know what drew you to this page, it wasn't just something. He's called the Holy Ghost (also known as the Holy Spirit).

You see, God is made of three persons: the Father, the Son (Jesus, fully God and fully man), and the Holy Spirit (who Jesus gave us not as a replacement, but as our comforter, who will come alongside us, while Jesus prepares a place for us, Heaven; until He comes back to earth and brings us with Him). To help you understand it in a much better context, it is like a triangle. Just like in the geometric shape, each part is connected. You might have already heard it said as the Trinity. God the Father, Jesus the Son, and the Holy Spirit have always been three separate persons. When we go to Heaven, we will see God, Jesus (sitting at the Father's right hand), and the Holy Spirit. In fact, when Jesus was on the earth and baptized by John, God the Father spoke to Him in the form of a dove. This scenario proves the Trinity is three separate persons.

And when Jesus was baptized, immediately He went up from the water, and behold, the heavens were opened to Him, and He saw the Spirit of God descending like a dove and coming to rest on Him; and behold, a voice from Heaven said, "This is my beloved Son, with whom I am well pleased." – Matthew 3:16-17 ESV

And through that triad, God put the urge inside you to reach the end of the book. Do you see it? God, the Maker of the Universe, all the stars and planets, and every living thing on earth, took the time to choose you! That, right there, is remarkable. God wants every person on earth to call on His Name, receive Him into their hearts, become saved, and go to their eternal reward, Heaven, to be with Him. However, regardless of how many people are called by God to be His, few hear the call, take action, and surrender their lives to Him.

For many are called, but few are chosen. – Matthew 22:14 KJV

But thank God you made your decision. You see, salvation takes faith. One of the main reasons some of us deny our faith soon after accepting Jesus is that we struggle with one area: proof. Not just evidence in the Bible, but of seeing Jesus with our own eyes—touching Him, feeling Him hold us close, hearing His voice—we struggle with knowing He is there. And it is hard to understand because we wish everybody else could see Him too. But, you see, that is not how faith works. The definition of faith is the exact opposite. According to *A Student's Dictionary*, it is a belief in something that is not seen, relying on trust. So, faith is not in what we can see, hear, touch, or feel. It is in what we can't.

That if you confess with your mouth the Lord Jesus and shall believe in your heart that God has raised Him from the dead, you shall be saved. For with the heart man believes unto righteousness; and with the mouth confession is made unto salvation. – Romans 10: 9-10 NKJV

All you must do is believe that Jesus Christ died on the cross, rose from the dead, and ask Him to come into your heart. And then, you will be saved! Pretty simple. So, let's do this together.

Lord, Jesus, I believe You died on the cross and rose again three days later. I repent of my sins and ask You to come into my heart and life. I make You my Lord and Savior. Thank You for forgiving me. In Jesus' Name, amen.

Now, you are born again. You just started your walk with Jesus. Mark this day on your calendar because you will want to remember this for the rest of your life. Okay, go ahead and celebrate, tell your friends and family, whatever you need to do. And don't forget to find yourself a faith, Bible-believing, full-gospel church. That is crucial. All of Heaven is rejoicing because you have just decided to fall into the arms of your Father. You are now saved and a son or daughter of the King.

ACKNOWLEDGMENTS

This book would not be possible without my Lord and Savior, Jesus Christ. Father, you have always been faithful. You did not give up on me. You had the confidence in me I didn't have in myself. Before anything regarding this book came to be, You gave me this gift. Lord, You get all the glory for it. I worship You, Jesus, And I will keep honoring You with my words until I have none left.

My mom, dad, and sister, Shannon, are the core of my support system with this long and extensive process, and they have been patient with me and there through it all. There were memories and mountains this season, and I am so thankful I did not do it alone. I cherish them more than anything.

My primary editor, Jaime McKinney, a professor at Regent University in Virginia Beach, Virginia, is a shining star. She is so busy, yet she took the time to edit this book, making every deadline with so much patience and diligence. She is full of faith, godly encouragement, and laughs. She is one of the best editors I have ever had, if not the best.

My second editor, Cristel Phelps, helped me craft this book for two years. She was so kind in encouraging me, giving me advice, and filling my head with wisdom on navigating as an author and an editor. She is truly something special.

My friend, Bishop H.O. "Pat" Wilson, was also a vital part of this book's process. It was when watching his sermon, "What Can 2 or 3 Do?" that I witnessed a tug in my Spirit and chose to willingly stand and be a catalyst for revival in my generation. He reminded me that I could do something for the Kingdom of God no matter how young I am, as long as I am willing to be His determined and surrendered vessel.

My wonderful and loving church family has not only supported me during this season, but they've been there for me since the beginning of my life. They never stopped encouraging me with advice, prayers, hugs, cards, notes, and letters. I consider it a privilege to have grown up with their influence, and I'll cherish them all my days.

My Pastor, Tim, is the most surprising contributor to this book. I remember hearing him call me a millennial, and a few days later, my teenage self had a plan to prove him wrong. Thankfully, God helped me turn away from immaturity, changed my course, and gave me this book instead. I am thankful to have him on my support team because he is determined despite his humanity. He leads with integrity and a humble heart. He models a life walking with Jesus while maintaining joy and a sense of humor. I praise God for his love and example.

It was a literal Godsend for James L. Rubart and Thomas Umstattd Jr. to give me much help, feedback, and information about my craft and the writer's market. Their time, prayers, effort, and patience in mentoring me meant more than they will ever know.

Christian author and speaker Jane Daly is a real person. I find myself joking about this because a few months after I met her, I asked one of my writing group's leaders if she wasn't a random stalker. Fortunately, he confirmed it, and Jane and I talked on the phone, joking about the cheeky misunderstanding. But all humor aside, Jane stepped up and gave me feedback about my premise, and helped me craft an entire book proposal. She is the bomb; much of my gratitude goes to her.

Mrs. G helped me learn my craft from the start, from the hamburger essay structure to non-fiction articles for the school newspaper. Her weekly lunch hour study and tutor sessions and her kindness helped me see the significance of writing and English in a way I hadn't seen before. I believe it is because of her dedication that I've become the author I am today. I will love and appreciate her always.

Mr. N reminded me to embrace opposition and not lose faith. And he helped me keep my focus on God and be

ACKNOWLEDGMENTS

in tune with the Holy Spirit, no matter how many voices I heard around me.

Mr. K showed me I didn't need to fit into the crowd to be accepted. In few words he encouraged me to not lose sight of who God made me to be and never compromise my beliefs, no matter what outside pressures come my way.

And finally, a big thank you to all of my book contributors. Those include my faithful beta readers, Becky, Jesse, Marita, and Andrew; my endorsers, Dan, Stephen, Tim, Edwin, Jane, Pat, and Paul (also to Sarah for being the go-between!); and my quote contributors, Luke and Roland. These bold men and women of God brought forth an extreme effort! I am so grateful for their patience, hard work, and encouragement to make this book happen.

ABOUT THE AUTHOR

A.M. REVERE has been bringing life to mere figments of her imagination ever since she could pick up a pencil. Growing up in a small church under the influence of intercessors, pastors, and evangelists, she has always been drawn to the Presence of God and unity of the Body of Christ in prayer, worship, and faith. And their godly example has helped shape the woman she is today. Her books show her roots, encapsulated into stories with sentimentality, tragedy, Christlike love, and tiny dashes of humor. She prays that God speaks to readers through her books and her mission statement—*Write. Touch. Impact. React.*— is brought to the surface in their lives.

End Notes

13th Amendment to the U.S. Constitution: Abolition of Slavery (1865). (1865). Retrieved from ourdocuments.gov: https://www.ourdocuments.gov/doc.php?flash=true&doc= 40

College, V. (2015). Passion for God [Recorded by D. E. Jr.]. Tulsa, Oklahoma, United States of America.

Cyrus, L. M. (2019). *Ode to Overload.* Nashville, Tenessee, United States.

Daugherty, P. (2017, November 16). *You Were Born to Fly* [MP4 file]. Retrieved from https://www.youtube.com/watch?v=Gh8h31TmZyo

Depew, Roland. "Week 6 Lecture." Old Testament II. Old Testament II, 2019, Tulsa, Victory College.

Gibson, Allison M, and Ed Yeager. "Sweet Child O'Mine ." *Reba*, season 6, episode 6, WB Network, 17 Dec. 2006.

Goodrich, Chauncey A, ed. "Carnal Definition & Meaning." Merriam-Webster. Merriam-Webster, 2022. https://www.merriam-webster.com/dictionary/carnal.

Goodrich, Chauncey A, ed. "Enemy Definition & Meaning." Merriam-Webster. Merriam-Webster, 2022. https://www.merriam-webster.com/dictionary/enemy.

Goodrich, Chauncey A, ed. "Millennium Definition & Meaning." Merriam-Webster. Merriam-Webster, 2022. https://www.merriam-webster.com/dictionary/millenium.

Goodrich, Chauncey A, ed. "Sin Definition & Meaning." Merriam-Webster. Merriam-Webster, 2022. https://www.merriam-webster.com/dictionary/sin.

Johnson, Joanna, Brad Bedeweg, and Peter Paige. Whole. *Good Trouble* Season 2. Burbank, California: Freeform, December 6, 2019.

Johnson, S. (1998). Who Moved My Cheese? New York City: G.P. Putnam's Sons.

Sharf, S. (2016, September 6). What Is A 'Millennial' Anyway? Meet The Man Who Coined The Phrase. *Forbes Magazine.*

Shelton, S. (2020, April 28). *The Filter of Promise* [MP4 file]. Retrieved from https://vimeo.com/413609920

Stein, J. (2013, May 20). Millennials: The Me Me Me Generation. *Time.*

Wiersbe, W. (2009). *Be Skillful (Proverbs): God's Guidebook to Wise Living.* Colorado Springs: David C Cook.